Foreword

BY FRANCES NEEL CHENEY

Associate Director, Peabody Library School

Experienced reference librarians learn, sometimes painfully, through years of service, that the reference act involves more than that indispensable knowledge of sources of information. They learn that the act is conditioned by the administrative policies of the library where it occurs, by the strengths and weaknesses of that library's resources, by the personalities of those seeking service and those giving it. All these things are talked about in library school courses in reference service, sometimes piously, sometimes fiercely, sometimes cursorily by those who want to hurry on to sink their teeth in the tough leather of bibliographies and indexes, dictionaries and encyclopedias, yearbooks and atlases, and all the other divers sources of stored information. But talk is not enough. Generalizations are not enough.

What is needed is specificity—meat and bones of specific cases, cases which come alive to the reader, which challenge him to exercise his judgment, formulate policies, plan courses of action in terms of a specific situation.

That is what we have in this series of cases, prepared and tested for validity during the past decade by Thomas Galvin, and now available for us to test our wits on, with Winchell at our side.

Read on, reader, for this book really needs no foreword, as

GOOD WINE NEEDS NO BUSH

v

PROBLEMS IN REFERENCE SERVICE

Case Studies in Method and Policy

PROBLEMS
IN REFERENCE
SERVICE

*Case Studies
in Method
and Policy*

By Thomas J. Galvin

Foreword by

FRANCES NEEL CHENEY

R. R. BOWKER COMPANY

New York 1965

Contents

Acknowledgments

The case study entitled "A Choice of Editions" appeared originally, under another title and in a slightly different form, in the *Journal of Education for Librarianship,* (Spring, 1963). Portions of the "Introduction" have also been adapted from material originally published there.

Many individuals have helped to make this book possible, but to none am I more deeply indebted than to Kenneth R. Shaffer, Director of the School of Library Science, Simmons College. Professor Shaffer was a pioneer in the application of the case method of instruction to library education. It was he who suggested to me, several years ago, that the method might be applicable in the beginning reference course, and subsequently, made it possible for me to carry on the instructional experiments of which this book is the result. Throughout this period, I have had the benefit of his experience, and the privilege of working with him while learning much from him.

I owe much, as well, to Professor Frances Neel Cheney, Associate Director of the Library School at George Peabody College, who has graciously contributed the "Foreword" to this book, and who has supported and encouraged the case experiment in reference teaching almost from its inception.

Special appreciation is due to Miss Sylvia A. Anderson who accomplished, with consumate skill, the task of preparing final manuscript copy for the book, and to Mr. John N. Berry III of the Book Editorial Department of the R. R. Bowker Company for advice and good counsel both before and during the period of manuscript preparation.

I wish to thank those students in the School of Library Science at Simmons College who have participated in the case experiment in the "Reference Methods" course and contributed many valuable suggestions. Other students, former students and professional associates, unfortunately too numerous to mention, have offered, out of their own experience, situations that ultimately found their way into case form. I am particularly grateful to Mrs. Dorrit Senior and Mrs. Judith Ekstrom for permission to include here solutions to case studies that they prepared originally in my classes.

Finally, I wish to thank William S. Rossiter and Mr. and Mrs. Martin T. Schumb for aid and encouragement both before and during the preparation of this book. Above all, in these and countless other respects, I acknowledge the unique contribution of my wife, to whom, with thanks and affection, this book is dedicated.

Simmons College
Boston, Massachusetts
November 1, 1964

Introduction

This book consists of 30 case studies in reference service along with two illustrative case analyses. The reader will find case studies here that emphasize the reference interview, many that are concerned with relating the reference inquiry to source materials, and still others involving the formulation or interpretation of reference policy. The settings vary from large research institutions to tiny branch libraries, and the participants from post-doctoral researchers to twelve year old children.

These cases are intended primarily for use in the formal academic training of librarians at the graduate level; more specifically in a general introductory or beginning course in reference method. It has been suggested that some might also prove useful in courses in library administration. One virtue of the case method, however, and of individual case studies, if the latter are properly constructed, is flexibility in terms of use. Thus, these case studies can be, and indeed, have been employed for other and less formal training purposes. Experience at Simmons College and elsewhere indicates that case studies such as these may also be used in a variety of post-graduate seminars, in-service training programs, and conference situations. Under such circumstances, a case study can provide a central focus of discussion for a group of individuals with varying backgrounds of experience and differing points of view towards reference service.

The case studies have been carefully chosen from a large body of case material prepared by the author over a period of approximately six years for use in the introductory reference course offered in the graduate program of the School of Library Science at Simmons College. During this period, a series of experiments was carried out in an effort to determine whether or not the case method of instruction might offer a more satisfactory means of achieving the objectives of the beginning reference course than do traditional teaching techniques. The results of these investigations indicate that the case method *is* applicable in this course, partly as a substitute for, and partly in combination with, conventional instruction. It is hoped that the publication of this collection may make it feasible for other teachers of reference to experiment with the case method.

In another context, I have discussed in some detail the objectives of an introductory reference course, the limitations of conventional teaching methods in achieving them, and the instructional values of the case method in this respect.* In brief, I should like to suggest that specific objectives of a beginning course in reference ought to include the acquisition of skill in analysis of reference questions and their relation to source materials, the provision of opportunities to learn the methodology of library research, and the development on the part of the student of a broad understanding of the range and variety of available informational resources. Moreover, it seems essential to focus attention on the complex human factors present in every reference situation which decisively influence its outcome.

Realistic preparation for reference service will take into account the fact that librarians operate in a variety of library situations, and that reference problems often must be solved with limited resources. It is equally important that an effort be made to overcome any artificial compartmentalization of librarianship that may be inherent in the library school curriculum, so that the prospective librarian is made to understand the relationship between the reference function and the library as a whole, and the role of the reference librarian both as a formulator and as an interpreter of administrative policy.

Critics of library education have focused attention on the limitations of the traditional "textbook-lecture-problem" method of teaching reference in achieving these objectives. Over-emphasis on the details of reference books, excessive memorization, use of class time to impart information that the graduate student ought perfectly well be able to obtain through independent study, failure to draw upon prior experience of students are among charges heard over and over again. Even more serious, it seems to me, is the de-humanization of the reference process and its reduction to a mechanical operation that is implied in this kind of instruction.

The traditional "problem" portion of the reference course consists of a series of exercises, each of which involves location of a single specific fact in some one of the reference sources currently under study. Substitution of case studies for such exercises grew out of a conviction that the traditional "problem" fails to provide an experience that is meaningful in preparing the student for the realities of reference service. Reference work consists fundamentally of three operations: first, finding out precisely what information is needed; second, determining the amount and kind of material required to provide this information and which, at the same time, the individual asking the

* "The Case Technique in Education for Reference Service," *Journal of Education for Librarianship*, Vol. 3, No. 4 (Spring 1963).

question is prepared to use effectively, and finally, locating the specific information in sources. The conventional "problem" omits the first two steps, and presents the student with merely the distilled end product of the reference art. The particular value of the case study as opposed to the "problem" is that it permits the incorporation within a single teaching vehicle of all elements of the reference encounter, including the reference interview and the solution of the reference question in terms of the strengths and limitations of a particular book collection. Thus, it more closely approximates the depth and sophistication of actual reference work, especially in its emphasis on the human factors involved.

Utilization of cases ends the artificial separation of the reference interview from the study of reference materials and search techniques. Broad generalization gives way to a consideration of the specifics of human behavior in complex and often confusing reference situations.

Reference policy has traditionally been presented in terms of lectures, required readings and, perhaps, class discussion based on these readings. Such abstract discussion of policy is of dubious value. There are no universally applicable rules. A policy that is correct and logical in one library situation may be quite indefensible in another. Yet, the lecture method of teaching makes it difficult to consider such matters except in terms of right and wrong.

The Case Studies

The 30 case studies in this book are intended to reflect some of the variety of kinds of problems that confront reference personnel in contemporary library situations. Experience with the case method in the beginning reference course indicates that it is possible to utilize as many as 20 case studies in a 15-week semester without unduly burdening students, still allowing ample time for the systematic examination of sources, most of which will occur outside of class. Similarly, it is quite possible to analyze this number of case studies in class, and have adequate time for presentation of essential background information about source materials by the instructor. It is assumed, however, that others may not wish to use cases quite so heavily, and that covering 15 cases in a semester course is perhaps more realistic. Thus, a book of 30 cases makes it possible to teach the beginning reference course in two successive semesters, or academic years, without duplication of assignments, or to instruct two sections of the course simultaneously, using different cases in each. To facilitate this, the case studies in this book that deal with reference sources are often paired. The book contains two case studies dealing with federal documents, two relating to statistical sources, etc.

It is perhaps appropriate to comment on the order in which the cases are arranged. A majority of the cases deal primarily with the relation of source materials to reference inquiries. Others are concerned largely with matters of reference and library policy, departmental administration, the ethics of reference service, and the like. These are interspersed throughout the text, rather than being grouped in any one place. This is done in order to avoid even the implication that reference policy is anything less than part and parcel of reference work as a whole. The policy cases do, however, follow a logical progression from rather narrow, well-defined questions about which a good deal has been written (such as the perennial problem of the contest addict), to larger and more complex issues.

The reader will also note that, in general, among the cases that involve utilization of sources to answer reference questions, those related primarily to bibliographical reference materials precede those related to the fact-finding type. The cases at the beginning of the book require chiefly the use of national and trade bibliographies, serial indexes, and the like, while those at the end more often involve encyclopedias, biographical dictionaries, almanacs, yearbooks and directories. This order is largely a matter of the author's personal preference in teaching the course, and there is no reason it cannot be altered. Those who do choose to begin with the fact-finding sources, however, will recognize the necessity of providing, quite early in the course, at least a brief introduction to basic indexes to professional literature, if students are to incorporate adequate documentation in their analyses of reference policy cases.

Each case study in this book is a record of a reference encounter in a library, and each has a basis in fact. It is important to emphasize, however, that in every instance the case studies represent composites. All facts, statistics, geographical and personal relationships have been radically altered, so that no case study contained herein can or should be identified with any single prototype. These cases, as presented, do not in any degree or sense portray any actual person, place, library or situation. All proper names are taken from the list entitled "Places in the U. S. with Populations Exceeding 2,500" which appears in *The World Almanac and Book of Facts for 1956* (pp. 266-281).

The reader will find some of these case studies rather lengthy. Quite naturally, the question arises as to whether it would not be possible to present the basic problem or issue embodied in a long case study in a briefer context. The answer is, of course, that it would be possible, but experience in teaching with cases indicates that a briefer presentation is rarely desirable. It is essential to the case method that problems be solved within the context of the specific library situation in which they arise. One must provide enough details about the environment in which a problem occurs, and allow the individual characters in the case to reveal themselves through dialogue, so that the student can get a clear sense of *what the specific situation is.* Failure to sketch out the circumstances surrounding a problem in some detail results only in vague, generalized or meaningless student solutions.

To illustrate the point, let us examine case eight, entitled "A Proposal to Purchase the Library of Congress Catalogs." The basic question embodied in this rather long case study might be phrased thusly: "Should an academic library, located in an institution devoted to the training of elementary and secondary school teachers, purchase the printed catalogs of the Library of Congress for its reference collection?" I would venture to suggest that the only possible answer to this question, stated in these terms, would be "it depends."

There are, of course, at the other extreme, obvious limits to how far the case writer can go in reproducing a real situation on paper. At best, the case study is no more than a mere *simulation* of reality, an approximation of an actual reference situation. It is not a substitute for experience that can be gained only through actually doing reference work in a library, but rather an instructional vehicle designed to prepare students for such a working experience in a more realistic and meaningful way. This group of case studies is not intended to reflect the content of a "typical working day" at a public reference desk. On the other hand, it does seem useful to point out again that these cases are not manufactured out of whole cloth. The experienced reference librarian will recognize many parallels here to real situations. The very frequency with which colleagues and students have claimed to be able to recognize the prototypes of these cases makes it clear that they are not wholly divorced from reality. In some instances, the author has had as many as half a dozen different individuals, each of whom insisted that he knew the real situation on which a particular case was based, and each of whom identified a different library as the setting.

A final word of caution is required for those who use this book instructionally. Almost every case study contains some material not directly relevant to the basic problem to be resolved, but deliberately inserted in order to provide an experience in identifying pertinent data for the student. Similarly, in an effort to develop a critical attitude on the part of the student, especially towards facts garnered through the reference interview, the cases may contain deliberate inaccuracies, misspellings, incorrect dates, and the like. Recognition of such inaccuracies will on occasion be crucial to the correct analysis of a problem, although every effort has been made to avoid, in this process, descending to the level of the "trick question."

The Case Method

Because the case method of instruction has been both widely discussed and frequently misunderstood, it seems important to attempt some clarification for the guidance of those who may wish to experiment with it in a teaching situation. Again, as with the preceding discussion of the reference interview, a prose description of teaching with cases is a poor substitute for the experience itself. It is difficult, for example, to communicate the very real atmosphere of excitement engendered when individual students, in presenting solutions to a case in the classroom, begin, quite unconsciously, to identify with the characters in the case. Moreover, it is not easy to generalize about the case method, because case studies themselves vary so widely one from another. Finally, teaching with cases is a highly personalized matter, and every instructor or group leader must seek and find his own *modus operandi*.

The case method of teaching reference is, however, based on certain fundamental assumptions. Among these is a belief that a basic aim of the course should be development of the skills of investigation, analysis, evaluation of evidence, decision making and reporting. A distinguishing feature of the case method is the extent to which the individual student is required to investigate a problem, weigh the facts, and arrive at a decision on his own.

As I have used case studies in the beginning course in reference methods, a fairly clear instructional pattern has emerged. Concurrently with the study of reference sources, which follows the usual "unit" plan, students are assigned cases to analyze, and an indication is made of the date on which each case will be discussed. In advance of that date, the student is required to determine for himself the amount and kind of information that, in his best judgment, is needed to provide an adequate response to the problems raised in the case, and then to proceed to locate all pertinent data. Each student comes to class on the day the case is to be discussed armed with a fully documented solution to the problem. Class time is devoted largely to presentations by one or more students, with group evaluation of each proposed solution. It should be clearly understood that, used in this way, the case study becomes considerably more than a mere device to stimulate class discussion.

Case studies do not lend themselves to pat "right or wrong" solutions, since in every instance there are at least two possible and eminently defensible answers, or methods of solving the problem. Satisfactory analysis of a reference case usually requires that the student consider several alternate courses of action before making a final decision as to the manner in which a particular problem is to be handled.

An examination of the illustrative analyses appended to the first two case studies in the book should serve to clarify this. Each analysis is reproduced here essentially in the form in which it was originally submitted in response to a classroom assignment, and each represents an adequate treatment of the problem with which the analyst is dealing. These samples are intended solely to indicate the depth of research and the amount and kind of documentation expected of students in a case method course at Simmons College, and the student is cautioned against attempting to employ them as models in the solution of other cases.

This kind of formal paper or report is required four or five times in a semester course. For the remainder of the cases, students are asked merely to prepare a set of notes or an *aide-memoire* in each instance, although it is important to note that these less formal analyses are expected to give evidence of a similar depth of research and careful documentation.

The first case presents a typical, elementary, bibliographic reference problem. Here, variety occurs chiefly in terms of methodology, since all students are proceeding towards a predetermined end in the form of "correct" answers to each of the questions raised by Mr. Lowell. The contents of the limited large edition of Shaw are either the same as the contents of the standard edition, or they are different. A collected edition of Shaw either has, or has not been published. These, presumably are matters, not of opinion, but of fact.

The difficulty lies, of course, in establishing the facts, and here is where the student is called upon to exercise judgment. At what point does one call a halt to the search for a collected edition? This, indeed, is a question to which there is no single "correct" answer, since it involves considerations of available time, identity of the inquirer, and importance of the inquiry. The length of time to be spent on a reference question is not subject to meaningful generalization, but the case study makes it possible to introduce this concept in a realistic context.

The second sample analysis deals with a problem requiring an administrative policy decision in the reference area. The solution proposed by the analyst is, as she has indicated, one of at least three possible answers that public librarians have found to the vexing problem of puzzle and contest questions. The proposed solution might easily be challenged, since it is possible to take and to defend the position that the reference librarian should locate the answers for this patron, or even that no reference aid at all should be given to this particular contestant. This case is intended particularly to illustrate the possible administrative implications of a decision to impose limits on reference service made by a subordinate officer of the library at a public desk.

It will be noted that each case study is followed by a series of questions. These are intended for the sole purpose of suggesting fairly obvious aspects of the case that might appropriately be explored by the student, although under no circumstances ought they limit the direction of any analysis. In my own classes, I have instructed students to ignore the questions at the end of any case, if they felt that other problems embodied in the situation were more deserving of attention. In the process of independent case analysis, students are free to explore any avenue of thought to whatever extent they judge appropriate, just as they are free to, and, indeed are encouraged to, draw on any source materials known to them individually. Professional literature, the literature of fields other than librarianship, or personal experience may be utilized fully and in whatever combination the individual deems best suited to the problems raised in a particular case study.

A Bibliographical Note

In addition to the journal article by the author cited earlier, several other books and articles may be useful for those who desire a fuller orientation to the case method. *Library Personnel Administration and Supervision* by Kenneth R. Shaffer (Shoe String Press, 1963) contains an excellent "Introduction" which describes in some detail the use of the case method in teaching library administration, and the role of the instructor in a case method course. The book also contains sample solutions of case studies, as does Professor Shaffer's earlier work, *The Book Collection* (Shoe String Press, 1961). Both of these books should be examined by anyone contemplating the use of case studies in a teaching situation. Another example of the presentation and analysis of an administrative problem in case form may be found in Henry Birnbaum's "The Case of Eulalia Brown" (*Library Journal*, October

15, 1958). The most useful general work on the case method that I have come across is *The Case Method at the Harvard Business School,* edited by Malcolm P. McNair (McGraw-Hill, 1954).

The case method is not offered as a panacea for the ills of library education in general. Neither will it solve all of the perennial problems of education for reference service. Its claims are more modest. It is my belief, and this belief is shared by some colleagues who have been associated with the experiments that led to the writing of this book, that instruction in the reference area is improved when case studies are used in combination with older and more widely accepted teaching methods. It is hoped that the availability of a collection of cases in reference method and reference policy may encourage faculty members in other library schools, as well as those responsible for postgraduate and in-service training of librarians, to conduct further experiments of this kind, and to report on the results to the profession. Should the book prove useful in this way, its author will consider himself well compensated for the effort involved in compiling it.

1 A Choice
of Editions

A_____ College is a growing liberal arts institution, located in a suburb of a large eastern city. Its enrollment has expanded since 1945 from 1,400 to 2,200 students. While the college continues to emphasize undergraduate study in the liberal arts and sciences, it has also begun to develop graduate programs in selected areas. At present, some 150 graduate students are enrolled as candidates for the degree of Master of Arts, chiefly in the fields of English and American literature, history, economics and art.

The college library occupies a spacious building, dedicated in 1959. The library's collections have grown rapidly in recent years, keeping pace with the demands of an expanded instructional program and increased enrollment. The book collection now numbers in excess of 160,-000 cataloged items, and is growing at the rate of approximately 3,500 titles annually. The library has a staff of 15, with seven professional librarians.

At A_____, as at many academic institutions, most recommendations for book purchases are initiated by the faculty. Although every member of the professional library staff is encouraged to submit recommendations for books to be added to the collections, only about ten percent of the library's purchases originate with the staff. Recently, members of the faculty and the staff have been asked to recommend for purchase both new titles and older works of major significance which are needed to meet the requirements of the new programs of study.

Charles Lowell, associate director of the library, is responsible for the acquisitions program. Mr. Lowell has organized the mechanics of this process carefully, so that the work of book purchasing can be carried on by a clerical assistant who prepares book orders for his signature after routine checks against duplication have been made. The present

1

clerical assistant is Mrs. Ruth Lenox, a college graduate, who has held this post for five months. Under Mr. Lowell's direction, Mrs. Lenox has developed into a particularly capable member of the staff.

Ethel Ogden is one of two professionally trained librarians comprising the reference staff at A_____. The library has a strong reference collection, including most of the notable bibliographic works of the 20th Century, such as the printed catalogs of the Library of Congress and British Museum, as well as major indexes to periodical literature.

One morning Miss Ogden arrived at her desk to find Mrs. Lenox waiting for her. After they had exchanged greetings, Mrs. Lenox explained the purpose of her visit:

"Ethel, we've run into a little puzzle that Mr. Lowell thought you might be able to help with."

"Why certainly. What is it?"

"Well, last semester Professor Ames in the English Department sent us this recommendation, suggesting that we buy Shaw's *Collected Works*."

Miss Ogden examined the purchase recommendation form, which is reproduced below.

Class No.	Author (surname first) *Shaw, Bernard*			
Accession No.	Title *Collected Works*			
No. of copies ordered				
Date ordered	Publisher and Place *Constable*			Year *1923(?)*
Dealer	Edition or series	Volumes	List Price	Cost *$150.*
Date received	Requested by *A. R. Ames*		Notify	
Date of bill	Reviewed in			
L. C. card No.	Approved by		Fund Charged	
GAYLORD 101-L				PRINTED IN U.S.A.

Mrs. Lenox continued: "Of course, I immediately checked the card catalog, to see if we already had this edition, and we didn't. Then I checked in *Books in Print*, but couldn't find it listed there. So, I put the card in the "out-of-print" file. The other day, I was going through this catalog, and I found these two sets listed."

Mrs. Lenox produced a dealer's catalog, and Miss Ogden examined the two entries reproduced below:

> 704. BERNARD SHAW, COMPLETE WORKS, The Limited Large Edition, Deluxe, from 1 to 30, orig. Green cloth, with all the Indexes and Bibl. London, Constable 1930
> $100.00

> 705. BERNARD SHAW, COMPLETE WORKS, Standard Edition, 34 vols., Including musical and Theatrical Criticisms, Constable & Co. $67.50

Mrs. Lenox continued: "I wasn't sure if either of these was the same as the *Collected Works* that Professor Ames wanted us to buy, so I asked Mr. Lowell. He said he didn't know either, and since the amount of money involved was considerable, he didn't want to make a mistake. You can see, the titles are different and so are the dates of publication and the prices."

"Why don't you just ask Professor Ames? He's the Shaw expert around here," Miss Ogden suggested

"That's just the problem. Ames is on sabbatical this semester. And if these sets are out-of-print, Mr. Lowell says we have to act fast if we don't want to lose the chance to pick them up."

"Would you like me to look into it, and see what I can find out?"

"Yes. Mr. Lowell said he has several questions that he hoped you could find the answers to. First of all, he'd like to know what the differences are between this Limited Large Edition and the Standard Edition. Is it just binding, or are the contents different? He also wants to know if either of these is the same as the Collected Edition, or if there actually is a Collected Edition. He wants to make sure that there hasn't been any better edition of Shaw published more recently. If we buy one of these, he wants to be certain we're getting the most complete and scholarly edition available."

Miss Ogden agreed that she would make some investigations, and report her findings to Mr. Lowell as soon as possible.

The solution to this problem lies in the preparation of a memorandum containing the answers to the specific questions raised by Mrs. Lenox. The memorandum should include citations to any pertinent references, in the event that Mr. Lowell wishes to examine any of these himself.

■ AN ANALYSIS OF CASE 1

BY DORRIT SENIOR

Memorandum from Miss Ogden to Mr. Lowell

SUBJECT: Request by Professor Ames to Purchase the Collected Works of Bernard Shaw.

Professor Ames submitted a recommendation that the library purchase the *Collected Works* of Bernard Shaw published by Constable in (?) 1923. The expected cost was to be $150. Mrs. Lenox has found two sets listed in a dealer's catalog . . .

> 704. BERNARD SHAW, COMPLETE WORKS, The Limited Large Edition, Deluxe, from 1 to 30, orig. Green cloth, with all the Indexes and Bibl. London, Constable 1930
> $100.00

> 705. BERNARD SHAW, COMPLETE WORKS, Standard Edition, 34 vols., Including musical and Theatrical Criticisms, Constable & Co. $67.50

. . . and is uncertain whether either of these might be the set that Professor Ames had in mind. They differ both from one another and from the set requested in title, year of publication and price.

Since Professor Ames, the logical person to consult as our Shavian authority as well as the person responsible for requesting the acquisition, is on sabbatical, I have attempted to ascertain the pertinent details regarding the two above works.

Professor Ames listed Constable as the publisher and both sets from the dealer's catalog were also listed as published by Constable. In fact Shaw had a warm relationship with this firm and they were the sole publishers in England of his works from 1903 until his death in 1950.[1] The firm published two separate collections of his works which included his novels, plays, essays and theatre criticisms.[2,3,4,5]

The first of these was a special limited luxury edition which was for purchase by subscription prior to publication. According to the publisher's prepublication releases this "event of outstanding importance in the literary world" was heavily oversubscribed.[6] This edition was limited to 1,025 copies; 1,000 were numbered 1-1,000, and 25 were lettered A-Y. Between 1930 and 1932, 30 volumes were published and three matching volumes were added. One was published in 1934, and two in

1938, thus completing the Limited Collected Edition totalling 33 volumes.[7] This edition has also been described as the Limited Edition, the Collected Edition, and appears to correspond to the Limited Large Edition listed as Item 704 in the dealer's catalog.

The Limited Collected Edition was printed in Caslon type on medium octavo 9″ x 6″.[8] The paper was specially made and the binding was jade green linen.[9] The edition was printed by R. & R. Clark of Edinburgh, and bound by Leighton-Straker Book-Binding Company. The green linen was manufactured at the request of Mr. Shaw by Morton Sundour Fabrics Ltd.[10] The price was one guinea (21/-) per volume but these were not sold singly, only as a set.[11]

The Standard Edition consists of 36 volumes. The publication of this edition commenced in 1931 and the last volume was added to the set in 1951.[12] This edition was not printed as a single collection, and each volume was sold individually at 6/- or 7/6 depending on its length.[13] It comprises the most complete collection of Shaw's writings. It contains not only all the writings present in the 33 volume Limited Collected Edition, but additional material as well which was only written and published after the completion of that earlier edition.[14]

The Standard Edition was printed in Fournier type entirely reset on extra crown octavo 8″ x 5″.[15,16] The paper was of excellent quality, and the binding was blood red (Venetian Red) linen cloth with gilt top and neat gold lettering. The prepublication announcements described it as "a delight to the eye, and a welcome addition to any library." [17] There have been many reprintings of these volumes over the years, all in the same format and type,[18,19] and at the present time all 36 volumes are still in print.[20,21]

Of interest is the existence of yet a third published collection of Shaw's works. This was published in America between 1930 and 1932. It consisted of 30 volumes matching the first 30 of the Limited Collected Edition published by Constable in England. The number was limited to 1,790 copies, but the three additional volumes of the English set were never added.[22,23,24]

It is apparent from the foregoing that neither of the items listed in the dealer's catalog is complete. The Limited Collected Edition (described in the catalog as the Limited Large Edition) should, if complete, total 33 volumes; and the Standard Edition 36 volumes. Since the Standard Edition is currently in print, there seems little purpose in purchasing a purportedly complete set which in fact lacks two volumes. As Professor Ames mentioned *Collected Works* and a price of $150 it suggests that he had the Limited Collected Edition in mind. Whether the particular set in the dealer's catalog, missing three volumes as it does, would satisfy Professor Ames is doubtful.

In carrying out this investigation of Professor Ames' request I consulted a number of other sources of information which further supported the above findings. As you might possibly wish to research further before coming to a final decision and to obviate a duplication of effort, I have listed these references in a Bibliography.

Notes

[1] James Shand, "Author and Printer. G.B.S. and R. & R. Clark 1888-1948," *Alphabet and Image: A Quarterly of Typography and Graphic Arts*, No. 8 (December, 1948), pp. 3-38.

[2] Arthur F. White, "Bernard Shaw," *Encyclopedia Americana*, 1959 ed., XXIV, 664-65.

[3] A. C. Ward, *Bernard Shaw*, V. I of *British Book News Supplements*, ed. T. P. Beachcroft (London: Longmans, Green & Co., 1951), p. 45.

[4] John D. Gordan, *Bernard Shaw 1856-1950: An Exhibition from the Berg Collection* (New York: New York Public Library, 1956), pp. 10, 13.

[5] National Book League of London, *A Catalog of an Exhibition celebrating the Ninetieth Birthday of Bernard Shaw* (London: Cambridge University Press, 1946), p. 7.

[6] "Works of Bernard Shaw," *Publishers' Circular and Booksellers' Record*, May 17, 1930, p. 677.

[7] *Book Prices Current 1952-56*, LXIV, 599.

[8] Shand, *Alphabet and Image*, No. 8, pp. 3-38.

[9] *Publishers' Circular* . . . , p. 677.

[10] National Book League of London, *A Catalog . . . of Bernard Shaw*, p. 7.

[11] *Publishers' Circular* . . . , p. 677.

[12] Ward, p. 45.

[13] "Standard Edition of Shaw," *Publishers' Circular and Booksellers' Record*, Oct. 31, 1931, pp. 540-41.

[14] Ward, p. 45.

[15] Shand, *Alphabet and Image*, No. 8, pp. 3-38.

[16] *Publishers' Circular* . . . , October 31, 1931, pp. 540-41.

[17] *Ibid.*

[18] Ward, p. 45.

[19] Shand, *Alphabet and Image*, No. 8, pp. 3-38.

[20] *Reference Catalogue of Current Literature*, 1961 (London: Whitaker, 1961), p. 928.

[21] Letter from Constable & Co., of London, May 14, 1963.

[22] *Cumulative Book Index, 1928-1932*, p. 1880.

[23] Library of Congress, *A Catalog of Books represented by the Library of Congress Printed Cards issued to July 31, 1942* (Ann Arbor: Edwards, 1945), CXXXVI, 211.

[24] George Bernard Shaw, *The Collected Works of Bernard Shaw* (Ayot St. Lawrence ed., New York: W. H. Wise & Co., 1930-32), 30 vols.

Bibliography

American Book Prices Current. LXVII (1960-61), 507.

Cumulative Book Index. 1928-1963.

Current Biography 1944. p. 614

Ghosh, J. C., and Withycombe, E. G. (comp.) *Annals of English Literature 1475-1950*. 2d ed. Oxford: Oxford University Press, 1961.

Hoffman, Hester R. (ed.). *The Reader's Adviser and Bookman's Manual*. 9th ed. New York: R. R. Bowker Co., 1960.

Kunitz, Stanley J., and Haycraft, Howard (eds.). *Twentieth Century Authors. A Biographical Dictionary of Modern Literature.* New York: H. W. Wilson Co., 1942.

Kunitz, Stanley J. (ed.). and Colby, Vinetta. *Twentieth Century Authors. 1st Supplement. A Biographical Dictionary of Modern Literature.* New York: H. W. Wilson Co., 1955.

Library of Congress, *A Catalog of Books represented by Library of Congress Printed Cards . . . to July 31, 1942.*

—— *Supplement 1942-1947.*

—— *Author Catalog 1948-1952.*

—— *National Union Catalog 1952-1955.*

—— *National Union Catalog 1953-1957.*

—— *National Union Catalog 1958-*

Manly, John M. and Rickert, Edith (eds.). *Contemporary British Literature.* 3rd ed. revised & enlarged. New York: Harcourt, Brace & Co., 1935.

Sampson, George. *The Concise Cambridge History of English Literature.* New York: Macmillan Company, 1941.

Shaw Review. Vols. II-V, 1959-62.

2 A Difference of Opinion

J_____ is a suburban community of 21,000, primarily residential in character, located in one of the New England states. The J_____ Public Library, established in 1892, now contains approximately 32,000 volumes. The Library is housed in a large, frame building, once the home of one of the town's wealthiest families. This building, which has long been crowded far beyond its capacity with books, imposes severe limitations on the quality and kinds of service the library is able to offer to the community.

The present director of the J_____ Public Library is Walter Putnam. Mr. Putnam's immediate predecessor, Miss Tewksbury, was town librarian for 38 years until her retirement. She had obtained her training on the job, and served the library and the community faithfully, although with little distinction. She was oriented toward the "custodial" school of librarianship, and often seemed to place undue emphasis on the strict enforcement of borrowing regulations and the maintenance of silence in the reading rooms. She did little or nothing to improve the physical facilities of the library, or to expand and strengthen its services during her long period of tenure.

Mr. Putnam, who is now in his second year as director of the library, is 35 years old. A graduate of the School of Library Science at Y_____ University, he had had six years of professional experience as an assistant in the reference department of one of the stronger and more progressive large public libraries on the east coast before coming to J_____. Under Mr. Putnam's leadership, the J_____ Public Library has developed fairly rapidly from a poorly supported, antiquated and generally forbidding institution to a modestly successful, comparatively strong, small public library. The library's financial support has increased from $2.18 to $3.50 per capita, thus making it possible to improve and expand the book collection by the acquisition of many of the better new titles of high literary quality, the purchase of several hundred works of an earlier date, and the removal from the shelves of more than 2,000 outdated and inactive titles. Mr. Putnam has devoted particular attention to a rejuvenation of the reference collection, which now includes some 400 titles, many of them relatively recent acquisitions. In addition, Mr. Putnam has been carrying on an intensive public relations program to educate the community to the needs of the library, and especially to the need for an adequate building. Although this last has produced little in the way of tangible results so far, there are some indications of the development of a climate of public opinion that might be favorable toward a new building in the near future.

The library has a staff of six full–time employees, in addition to the director, all of whom are women, and none of whom have had any academic training in librarianship. With two exceptions, no member of the staff has had formal education beyond high school. One of the exceptions is Mrs. Barre, the reference librarian. Mrs. Barre is 43 years old, and is married to the local superintendent of the county power and light company. She is a college graduate, and was, before her marriage, an elementary school teacher. Since her children are approaching college age, Mrs. Barre has had to find a means to supplement her family income. Not wishing to return to teaching, she sought employment at the public library.

Mr. Putnam, faced with the problem of replacing a reference librarian who had retired, and aware that it would probably be impossible to attract a library school graduate to this position at the salary he was able to offer, decided that Mrs. Barre was the best qualified person available for the appointment. During the six months she has been a member of the staff, Mrs. Barre has seemed to fulfill most of the requirements of the position adequately. She has a fairly sound knowledge of basic factual reference sources, and is sufficiently skilled in their interpretation to be able to help people locate information. In addition, she has read widely and intelligently in the general book collection, and this is reflected in the readers advisory aspects of her work. Although Mrs. Barre seems to have a genuine desire to assist people toward more effective use of library resources, this is occasionally tempered by a suggestion of impatience when dealing with patrons who do not grasp facts or directions quickly. This impatience has been especially apparent in relationships with other members of the library staff. The fact that she tends to react in a highly emotional way at any suggestion of criticism has deterred Mr. Putnam from dealing with the problem of her adjustment to the library situation as decisively as he might have wished. He feels, however, that this is a fairly minor limitation, which he hopes will solve itself in time without any interference on his part.

One morning, as Mr. Putnam was working in his office, preparing a report for the coming meeting of the board of trustees, he was interrupted by the arrival of an unannounced visitor. The middle-aged, and not particularly attractive woman who entered, or rather "stormed into" his office, gave every indication of being extremely angry about something.

"Are you the librarian?"

"Yes, my name is Putnam. How may I help you?"

"You can begin by telling me what kind of service you are giving to the taxpayers around this place."

"Well now, first of all, won't you sit down, Miss . . ."

"Reedley. It's Mrs. Reedley."

"Mrs. Reedley, if you don't mind my saying so, you seem quite upset. Wouldn't you like to sit down over here?"

"Listen! I didn't come in here to chew the rag. I just want a few simple answers."

"Well, I'm afraid I can't be helpful unless you can tell me more specifically what the problem is."

"The problem is, Mr. Putnam, that I came into this library for some of that research service that you've been talking so much about in the papers, and when I got here, I find that there's no one who's willing to give me any help."

"Why, Mrs. Reedley, I'm very surprised to hear that. Now, Mrs. Barre . . ."

"Don't tell me about Mrs. Barre. She's the one I'm talking about. I'm doing some research that's very important to me, and she just refused to give any help at all. Now, my husband and I pay taxes in this town, and I intend to get the service that I'm entitled to."

"Mrs. Reedley, we certainly want to give you every reasonable library service that we can. Now if you'll just calm down . . ."

"Don't tell me to calm down. I can see that I'm wasting my time with you. I have a very good friend on the board of trustees. You haven't heard the last of me by any means. I'll just take this up with Mrs. Ayer."

Mrs. Reedley departed from the office as abruptly as she had arrived, leaving Mr. Putnam slightly angry and very puzzled. Her reference to Mrs. Ayer was particularly disturbing, since Mrs. Ayer was the least progressive of the six members of the library's board of trustees, and was inclined to be highly critical both of Mr. Putnam and of his operation of the library. He decided to talk immediately with Mrs. Barre, and to find out more about the altercation that had apparently occurred between her and Mrs. Reedley. Accordingly, he went to the reference desk, and asked Mrs. Barre to come to his office to discuss the matter.

Mrs. Barre appeared to be almost as upset as Mrs. Reedley had been. She explained that Mrs. Reedley had arrived at her desk with several contest questions taken from a series that had recently been appearing in the local newspaper. These involved determining the names of prominent Americans on the basis of isolated biographical facts which the newspaper supplied. She indicated that Mrs. Reedley had asked her to look up the answers to these questions for her, and to identify the people described. Mrs. Barre had responded that she would be quite willing to suggest possible reference sources Mrs. Reedley might use to locate the answers for herself, but that it would not be possible to take the time necessary to find the information for her. Mrs. Barre pointed out to Mr. Putnam that the latter could have required several hours of work, and that she felt this was not a proper kind of activity for members of the staff. At this point, Mrs. Reedley had apparently become abusive, and Mrs. Barre had responded, she admitted, a bit more sharply than she perhaps should have. Mrs. Barre was close to tears by the time that she finished recounting the episode for Mr. Putnam. She stated that she would not, under any circumstances, provide the answers to contest questions, either for Mrs. Reedley or for anyone else, and that she felt it was "ridiculous" to waste staff time in this kind of activity. Indeed, Mrs. Barre said that if answering contest questions for people like Mrs. Reedley was a part of her job, she would prefer some other type of work in the library, or else would resign from the staff rather than to have to perform this service.

Mr. Putnam indicated that he agreed with Mrs. Barre, at least in principle, that this type of question was not one to which large amounts of staff time should be devoted. He suggested that the library should perhaps have some policy approved by the board of trustees which would cover situations of this kind, and asked that Mrs. Barre direct any future inquiries along these lines to him.

After Mrs. Barre left his office, Mr. Putnam realized that the events of the morning might easily develop into an uncomfortable situation involving the board of trustees. He knew that poor public relations at this point, or a clash with the board, might jeopardize the immediate future development of the library, and the plans for a new building. He suspected that Mrs. Reedley would make good her threat to contact Mrs. Ayer, and that she might find in Mrs. Ayer a very sympathetic listener. He felt that, under the circumstances, he must prepare himself for the possibility that the matter might be discussed at the impending meeting of the board. On the other hand, his experience in the reference department at the M_____ Public Library had made him aware that answering contest questions could impose a real burden on the staff of a public library. He decided to investigate the policies of other libraries in dealing with contest and puzzle questions, and to prepare a full report on this subject for the board, to be accompanied by a statement of recommended policy for the J_____ Public Library.

The solution of this case consists of the preparation of a report on the problem of handling contest questions in the reference department of a public library, and a statement of recommended policy for the J_____ Public Library. Your analysis might also include a consideration of ways in which the unpleasant situation described here might have been avoided, as well as suggestions for any other course of action that Mr. Putnam or Mrs. Barre might undertake in order to resolve the problem in this specific instance.

■ AN ANALYSIS OF CASE 2

BY JUDITH EKSTROM

I. A Memo to the Board of Trustees from the Librarian

A member of our community recently visited the library in search of answers to contest questions. It has been my experience that a library is wise to have a stated policy on such matters so that patrons will be aware of what services the staff may reasonably be asked to perform and so that each case is not resolved by an individual decision. I would, therefore, like to call the attention of the board to the problem of answering contest questions and to an examination of what other libraries have done to meet the problem.

During the 1930's and 1940's, when the contest and puzzle craze was reaching its peak, librarians were probably much more sympathetic to contestants than they are today. It was soon discovered, however, as hordes of seekers descended upon the public library, that staff time was inefficiently squandered in performing time-consuming reference work, that expensive reference sets were mutilated or stolen, and that normal service to regular patrons was seriously disrupted. The literature of librarianship is filled with accounts of such happenings in libraries of all sizes, spread across the country. In evidence of this, I should like you to read a letter submitted to the editors of *Publishers' Weekly* in 1956 by the then Chief Librarian of the Brooklyn Public Library:

Editors; the *Publishers' Weekly*:

Puzzles have plagued libraries for years. Eager prize winners with their eyes on thousands of dollars, become ardent library enthusiasts for the period of the contest. The mutilation of valuable reference books is appalling. Books disappear from the shelves and are frequently lost forever to the library community because many of them are out of print.

Librarians have scant time to devote to the needs of people with far more important questions. The task of policing the desired reference books takes all their time and energy. Regular readers find that service is being interfered with and often leave in high dudgeon feeling that the library is at fault for allowing such goings on.

Most of the city's newspapers have been involved in these contests so damaging to the book collections of the libraries. We turn to you for help, therefore, in marshalling public opinion, not against our daily newspapers, of course, but against the type of contests which sends hordes of conscienceless individuals into the libraries to destroy the property held there in trust for the use of all people.

Last year this is what happened in the Brooklyn Public Library during puzzle contests:

89 atlases, dictionaries and encyclopedias were lost, 53 were so mutilated as to require replacement.

Uncompensated losses totaled $2,843.69. A total of 143 volumes had to be replaced. Many others could not be replaced.

Normal service to regular library users was seriously disrupted. Many research workers gave up trying to do their work. Staff members' nerves were frazzled.

Our public librarians work hard and conscientiously to operate within the limited funds available. The losses incurred during these unbridled puzzle contests, and the immense damage to the libraries' prestige, should be understood by the people whose taxes support them.

We earnestly hope you will help form a body of public opinion that will curb the Puzzle Nuisance for good and all.

Francis R. St. John
Chief Librarian
Brooklyn Public Library[1]

In investigating the practices of other libraries in handling this problem, I have found that there are three general schools of thought which we may consider.

The first school attempts to offer unlimited help, by endeavoring to answer all questions. Such libraries are usually characterized by adequate staff and have a philosophy of unlimited aid to all patrons. In an effort to preserve their collections, sometimes they even go to the extent of posting the answers to contest questions or publishing them in the newspaper. Such practices, though, lead inevitably to questions of ethics. The library may feel that contest workers are taxpayers and that their claims upon the library to help them better their economic status are just as valid as any wage earners. They point out that a so-called "noble purpose" for visiting the library is not a prerequisite. There is also the justification that service given the contest worker, who probably visits the library rather infrequently, may influence him to become a genuine library patron and supporter.

At the opposite end of the spectrum are those who deny any service at all to contest workers. These libraries usually feel that such service is not their responsibility and that it allies them with discreditable advertising gimmicks. They point out that users gain no learning from a search conducted by the librarian and remain ignorant of the processes of research. These libraries thus sidestep their educational role in the community. They are determined that a few users shall not impose their needs upon the entire community, and finally, they point to the enormous cost to the library in reference material and in staff time.

Between these two extremes is a middle ground that many libraries have sought in order to avoid alienating the contest worker, while at the same time not interrupting normal service. Their usual method is to point out to the contest seeker possible sources of information and attempt to educate the contestant by allowing him to conduct the search himself. Occasionally, safeguards of time limits or restrictions on use are introduced when demands become excessive, to ensure fairness to all and to preserve material. Such a policy has been adopted in the past by the Enoch Pratt Free Library in Baltimore:

> Although no time can be given to searching for information which answers contest questions, assistants should remember that in meeting contest workers they have an opportunity to introduce reference tools and to explain the elements of reference self-service to a new group eager for help and often quite ignorant of the resources of the Library. Assistants should explain that it would be unethical for the Library to answer the actual questions, but should be quick to suggest possible sources for the information. Whenever possible, groups of books are placed on reserve for the duration of the contest. Telephone inquiries should be discouraged, the assistant suggesting that the patron come to the Library and consult the appropriate material.[2]

Within the range of these three positions, various libraries have adopted specialized techniques which may be of interest. One library, which attempts to offer unlimited service, contacted the sponsor of the contest and pointed out to him that the library was forced to bear the costs, in lost and mutilated books, of providing answers. Since the sponsor was awarding prizes amounting to a considerable cash sum and was in addition profiting greatly from the advertising, it seemed fair that he underwrite the cost to the library. In this instance, the sponsor, a newspaper, willingly agreed.

A technique used successfully in some libraries has been to set aside pertinent material in a room or a corner designated for contest workers. They are thus provided convenient access and are prevented to a certain extent from disturbing other patrons. In addition to information sources, this area may contain a bibliography or the sources themselves on contest literature. Here the worker may find information on subjects such as his chances of winning, the legitimacy of the contest, the taxes on winnings and the problems that contests may cause to the public library.

Whatever regulations the library has decided to adopt are usually posted prominently as the formal policy. A courteous refusal of certain services will thus be supported by stated rules which the patron may examine. The library is protected from favoritism or charges of it.

I therefore consider it of value that the board take some of these questions of reference policy under consideration. In view of this I have prepared the above synopsis of the problem, so that it may be freely discussed. In order to provide some starting point, I should like to suggest a tentative policy which I, personally, think might have some value in our situation. The problem here is fortunately not acute, in terms of total expenditure, but it is necessary for us to be able to cope with such a situation if and when it should occur. I hope that any policy adopted by the board may be considered an experimental one until we have determined its fitness and adaptability to our particular situation.

I feel that as a medium-sized public library we ought to seek that middle-of-the-road which will enable us to provide adequate service to the contestant and yet not place a burden on the time of our reference workers. I, therefore, recommend the following:

> Please do not ask the librarians to find answers to contest questions or puzzles. We feel this is not an ethical or fair service to provide. The staff will be happy to direct you to sources where you may find the information yourself.

During periods when many persons visit the library to find contest information, the staff will endeavor to gather all pertinent material together in the reference room where you can find it easily.

Since the library does not provide direct answers to contest workers, we cannot answer such questions over the telephone.

II. Some Aspects of the Situation for Mr. Putnam to Ponder

1. On his relationship with Mrs. Barre and other library workers: This situation provides a convenient place to stop and take stock of the relationship between the librarian and his employees. It may be suspected that Mr. Putnam has so concentrated upon improving the library quality and facilities that he has neglected to provide the administrative leadership necessary to a well-functioning staff. He must remember that Mrs. Barre and the other ladies are not professionally trained, and it is, therefore, his responsibility to see that they get as much on-the-job training as he can provide. He has noticed the problem before, but has taken no action. Now is the time for him to put himself on a new footing with his staff.

"Lack of qualified personnel," says Alice Bryan in *The Public Librarian*, "was most frequently mentioned as the worst feature in the librarian's relation to the public." "Qualified" means being well trained and guided on the job, in addition to being library-school trained. The quality of our public service is certainly dependent to a large extent on our personal satisfaction in our work. Personal satisfaction is also reflected largely in public relations in whatever way that function may be different from public service. Some of the ills we now blame entirely on our low salaries and limited budgets may be caused as much by the confusion that comes from lack of imaginative assistance and the frustration that comes from lack of guided development as by poor financial arrangements. This has been found to be true in other fields of work, and surely, librarians are human beings too. It may be especially true in small libraries where the librarians have almost no contact with others doing the same work.[3]

2. On the policy to be adopted: Since the J_____ Public Library has not suffered from an influx of contest information seekers, any policy selected will probably cover isolated cases, as the one described. It probably does not matter much which policy the board finally selects —the important point is that the reference librarian have something to which she can point as legitimate grounds for refusing service in cases where the search might involve a great deal of time. Mr. Putnam may

decide to recommend the policy stated in his memo for two reasons; (1) it is the least controversial and will probably encounter the least opposition from the Board and, (2) since Mrs. Barre feels so strongly about the point, it may be just as well to recommend a policy which might be acceptable to her.

3. On Mr. Putnam's relationship to the board: Mr. Putnam is undoubtedly very wise in presenting the problem before the board confronts him. In doing so, he is maintaining his professionalism in preserving the proper relationship between the board and the librarian: "Complaints from the public are first the responsibility of the librarian and failing solution there, should be taken up at a meeting of the entire board." [4]

Mrs. Reedley, the complainant, and Mrs. Ayer, the unprogressive member of the board, have probably passed the point of listening to calm reasoning. Mr. Putnam should pursue them no further, unless they show signs of willingness to be persuaded. Instead, he should direct his whole effort to forestalling the spread of their dissatisfaction. By presenting his memo, he has, so to speak, initiated the first punch.

Throughout the discussion, he should try to avoid the board's focusing on the particular incident in the J_____ Public Library. The letter from the Brooklyn Public Library is designed to do just that— to present the problem of contest workers without bringing in J_____'s particular situation. In order to strengthen his position, both the memo and Mr. Putnam's remarks are aimed to point up the cost and inefficiency to the library.

As a regular procedure, Mr. Putnam would be wise to keep the board occupied in the months preceding the building of the new library with minor questions of policy. The technique of asking for experimental policies may avoid an irretrievable situation and enable him to adopt new policies for the new library.

> The most effective board-librarian relations are found in the libraries where the librarian keeps the board so well-supplied with interesting policy matters that it has little or no time for details.
>
> One librarian reports considerable success with the practice of asking that such policies be considered experimental. This gives the librarian an opportunity to report further and does not commit the library to a policy which might in the long run prove disadvantageous.[5]

After the board has decided upon a policy, Mr. Putnam might suggest that it be publicized, perhaps in the town paper, as well as posted in the library building. By presenting a brief summary of problems which contest workers may present to the library and by stating the

J_____ Public Library's policy, he may forestall criticism from the general public with whom Mrs. Reedley or Mrs. Ayer may have influence.

Notes

[1] "Curb the Puzzles Nuisance for Good and All," *Publishers' Weekly*, October 29, 1956, p. 2031.

[2] Enoch Pratt Free Library, *Staff Instruction Book* (Baltimore, 1935), no. 576.

[3] Phyllis Osteen, "Creative Supervision," *Wilson Library Bulletin*, XXVII (April, 1953), 629-32.

[4] Zelia J. French, *Library Management Handbook for Kansas Board Members* (Topeka, Kansas: Kansas Traveling Libraries Commission, 1962), p. 12.

[5] E. W. McDiarmid and John McDiarmid, *The Administration of the American Public Library* (Chicago: American Library Association and the University of Illinois Press, 1943), pp. 40-41.

III. *Additional Documentation*

A. Policies in other libraries:

"Contests," *Routine Book* (Carnegie Library of Pittsburgh), October 10, 1949, no. 20.

> Because of the frequent requests during a contest, the Library is unable to take the time to search for answers to contest questions. However, it must be remembered that an opportunity may present itself to introduce reference tools to a new group of borrowers, and assistants should take this opportunity to suggest possible sources for the information. Telephone inquiries are discouraged, but a suggestion may be made to the inquirer to come to the library to consult appropriate material. (Groups of books may be put on reserve for the duration of the contest.)

"Quiz Questions and Contests," *Staff Manual* (Racine Public Library), 1952, no. 91.

> Time should not be given in searching for an answer to a contest question but assistant should suggest possible sources for the information and make that material available. We should remember that in meeting a contest worker we have an opportunity to introduce reference tools and to explain the elements of reference self-service to a new group eager for help and often quite ignorant of the resources of the library.

B. Need for formal policy:

Margaret Hutchins, *Introduction to Reference Work* (Chicago: American Library Association, 1944), pp. 173-176.

Whenever it is necessary to refuse reference services, it should be done courteously, with an explanation of the reasons . . . A printed explanation of the rules, which may be handed or pointed out to the inquirer, will help to make the refusal more palatable.

Printed or typed rules may allay suspicion on the part of an offender that a rule has just been made up for his special annoyance. It is a generally accepted psychological principle that rules should be phrased in positive rather than negative terms so far as possible.

In order to prevent favoritism, or charges of it, it is advisable to make and enforce rules and regulations concerning questions which may and may not be handled by the reference department and concerning the relations between readers, the reference librarians, and the books. The most important prerequisite for making just and practicable rules for the governing of relations with and between the readers is to remember that the primary purpose of the reference department is to help the public.

C. Some general statements concerning a policy.

E. W. McDiarmid, "Library Needs Which Should Be Met," *Library Trends,* III (October, 1954), 113.

> . . . what society needs most from the library should not be determined by the individual request of established or prospective library patrons. That is to say, the library should not be a place where any citizen can come and find anything he or she wants. It should be a place where society, acting through its regularly constituted channels, has decided what its members most need and what if provided from among these needs will best serve to improve society.

Margaret Hutchins, *Introduction to Reference Work* (Chicago: American Library Association, 1944), p. 175.

> Many reference departments will not knowingly answer questions for contestants or bettors either over the telephone or in person. In some public libraries, however, assistance is given freely to people who are working on a contest for a prize on the grounds that their claims on the library to help them better their economic status are just as good as those of any wage earner. This argument is usually put forth in the smaller, more leisurely libraries, where helping people to solve puzzles and answer quiz contests does not interfere with other work nor put undue strain on reference materials.

Dorothy Huston, "More About Contests," *Library Journal,* April 15, 1941, p. 318.

> As long as the contestants do not mutilate books and require very little of the staff's time, we feel that they have a right to use the library. It does seem a shame to have valuable reference material

used for contests, but after all we do not demand of a library patron that he shall come to the library only for noble purposes.

Katharine Shorey, "In Defense of Puzzle Fans," *Wilson Library Bulletin*, XV (June, 1941), 866.

All the intelligence and all the effort and all the money expended on getting the new borrower into the Library will be dependent on some inner urge within the borrower himself, and no amount of Library propaganda will be as effective as one grain of inner necessity, as one moment of personal determination to go to the Library for help.

3 A Question
of Value

Martin Brentwood is reference librarian of the B_____ Public Library, which is located in a city of 160,000 on the eastern seaboard. Originally founded in 1884 under the auspices of the B_____ Literary Circle, the library early attracted the interest of some of the first families of the city. During the period from 1890 to 1930, many gifts of books were received from the personal collections of individuals who were prominent in the community. Among these was a large group of books, manuscripts and memorabilia which has since come to be known as the "Colton Collection."

Charles Colton settled in B_____ in the late 19th century. Beginning as a dry goods merchant, he soon entered the banking business, which, along with a variety of real estate ventures, ultimately made him quite a wealthy man by local standards. In his later years, Colton became an avid collector of books and manuscripts of all sorts. He was wholly unselective in his acquisitions, and was reputed to be an easy mark for every second-hand book dealer in the region. Colton was both an eccentric and something of a recluse, and since his collection was generally considered worthless by knowledgeable people, it is not surprising that he was rebuffed when he offered, shortly before his death, to present it to nearby S_____ University. In any event, the material ultimately found its way to the B_____ Public Library where it was stored for nearly 20 years in packing cases in the library basement.

In 1939, George Randolph, a young historian, was engaged in indexing a collection of local newspapers owned by the library, as part of a federally financed WPA project, when he chanced upon the Colton papers. Among the mass of unsorted material, Randolph found several manuscript diaries and ships' logbooks dealing with the early maritime

21

history of the region. He was able to utilize this unique and hitherto unknown collection as source material for a doctoral dissertation and, since he was a gifted writer, to produce as well an historical novel based on the documents. The novel was an instant success, and the "Colton Collection," on which it was based, became almost overnight a focus of considerable local pride and national interest.

Although he has made no effort to expand library holdings in the area of maritime history, Harold Blakely, the director of the B_____ Public Library, has been most astute in capitalizing on the Colton Collection as a means of achieving community interest in and support for his general program of library development. Immediately after his arrival at B_____, he succeeded in persuading a rather conservative board of library trustees to launch a campaign for funds to build an addition to the central library, ostensibly to create a suitable area to house the collection. In 1952, the new wing, financed through a combination of public funds and monies obtained by private subscription, was opened. This contained, in addition to a small but handsomely appointed Colton Room, a new adult reading room, a public service area for the reference department, and an audio-visual suite. All of these services had been badly overcrowded in the original building.

Martin Brentwood came to B_____ in 1956 as a professional assistant in the reference department, immediately after his graduation from library school. In 1958, Mr. Brentwood became reference librarian, and he now administers a department staffed by two professional assistants, as well as a third person who is enrolled as a student in a nearby school of library science on a part-time basis.

Brentwood is 38 years old, and holds a master's degree in economics as well as in library science. After completing his graduate studies in economics, he taught at a small liberal arts college before entering the library profession. Although his interests lie chiefly in the field of business and economics, Brentwood has had a sound general education in the liberal arts, is familiar with and appreciates fine books, and is an accomplished amateur musician. He enjoys his work at B_____, and likes the variety associated with reference service in a fairly busy and well patronized public library. The reference collection at B_____ is a good one for a library of this size and, because of the Colton Collection, is especially strong in bibliographic sources. The specialized resources at S_____ University, a few miles to the south, are also available to Mr. Brentwood for the occasional reference question which cannot be answered from sources available at B_____.

Brentwood has concentrated on improving and expanding the library's reference services to the community. He has been instrumental in developing close working relationships with high school librarians in the city, which have resulted in a cooperative program of instruc-

tion for students in the use of library resources and in further cooperation in the acquisition of specialized materials. Brentwood has also
made many contacts with business and professional people, and as a
result, he is frequently called upon to provide information to some of
the more important firms and individuals of B_____. As an incidental
aspect of his work, Mr. Brentwood has had primary responsibility for
the Colton Collection. Since this is not a collection to which materials
have been added with any degree of regularity, this responsibility has
involved chiefly supervision and maintenance. In the course of assisting
many of the individuals who visit the library to use this collection, he
has managed to familiarize himself rather thoroughly with the materials in the Colton Room. Although he has sufficient competence to
perform this task adequately, Brentwood has not developed any particular interest in the problems of special collections work.

Late one afternoon, as Mr. Brentwood was completing a period of
duty at the public reference desk, he received a telephone call from a
Miss Ethel Westerly. Brentwood had met Miss Westerly previously at
the library, since she was a frequent visitor. In the course of these
meetings, Miss Westerly had often talked with Mr. Brentwood about
her interest in the Colton Collection. Brentwood recalled that Miss
Westerly had, on several occasions, mentioned that her family had
been acquainted with Mr. Colton although, as might be expected of
an elderly person, she was somewhat cloudy in her recollection of the
details of this acquaintance.

During their telephone conversation, Miss Westerly indicated that
she had recently come across a rather interesting old book in her
father's library. She said that, knowing Mr. Brentwood's interest in
older books, she thought he might like to have an opportunity to
see it. Mr. Brentwood replied that he would, of course, be delighted
to see the volume in question, and suggested that she stop in at his
office when she next visited the library. Miss Westerly said that she
would be downtown the next day and that it would be most convenient
for her to see Mr. Brentwood at that time. Accordingly, an appointment
was arranged for the following afternoon.

At the appointed time, Miss Westerly appeared in Mr. Brentwood's
office. After an exchange of greetings, the conversation continued as
follows:

"Mr. Brentwood, I know you are a busy person, and I don't want to
take up too much of your time. But, the other day, I was going through
some of father's things, and I came across this unusual old book."

"Oh, yes. May I look at it?"

"It's really quite fragile, as you can see. Since it is so old, I thought
that it might be valuable."

"Well, of course you realize, Miss Westerly, that age isn't always very meaningful in determining the value of a book."

"Is that so? I didn't know that. Of course, I don't even know if I would want to sell it. I really just thought it might be interesting to find out whether or not it had any value. Actually, you know, I'm not even sure where the book came from. For all I know, this might even be a book that was originally part of Mr. Colton's library."

Mr. Brentwood examined the small volume, bound in a torn, slightly yellowed paper wrapper. Opening the book carefully, he immediately discovered that it lacked a title page, although indeed there was no indication that a title page had ever existed. The only bibliographic information which the volume contained was found on the outside of the paper jacket. This read as follows:

MAGGIE
A Girl of the Streets
(A STORY OF NEW YORK)
By
JOHNSTON SMITH
Copyrighted

In spite of the fact that he spent several minutes examining the book rather carefully, Mr. Brentwood was unable to discover any additional bibliographic information beyond the fact that it was 163 pages long. His first thought was to refer Miss Westerly to a dealer who would be able to appraise the volume's possible value, but he knew that the city of B_____ did not have any shops that dealt exclusively in older books. He was also aware that Miss Westerly might have difficulty in obtaining a free appraisal by mail unless she were prepared to offer the book for sale. Accordingly, he suggested that Miss Westerly leave the book with him for a few days, and indicated that he would be willing to try to determine what value, if any, it might have.

If you were Mr. Brentwood, outline in detail the steps you would take and the specific sources you would consult in order to locate information about this volume. Is it a first edition? What price might a dealer pay for it? What dealer or dealers would you suggest Miss Westerly contact if she should wish to dispose of this book?

Comment on the way in which Mr. Brentwood handled this problem. Are there any questions of policy involved in dealing with reference inquiries of this kind?

4 Two Unpublished Plays

K_____ College is an undergraduate institution which emphasizes the liberal arts. It is located in a large southeastern state, and is a campus college approximately 25 miles from the nearest large city. It has an enrollment of nearly 2,500 undergraduate men and women, as well as about 150 graduate students in art, literature, and the social sciences. The college has been fortunate in that it is able to offer a rich and varied academic experience to its students, and can also provide facilities that would be far beyond the means of the average institution of comparable enrollment and size. Many distinguished teachers and scholars have been attracted to its faculty, and it would be unusual indeed if at any given time K_____ could not also boast of at least one or two important authors, composers, or artists in residence.

The excellent quality of the K_____ College Library has been a major factor in making it possible for the college to attract and retain its splendid faculty. The library is exceptionally well supported, and has been the recipient of many gifts, both of money and of interesting, unusual, and rare materials. It has a small, carefully selected collection of rare books and manuscripts which is maintained and serviced with great skill by one particularly talented member of the staff. The library has nearly 250,000 cataloged volumes as well as sizable resources in uncataloged documents.

The staff of the reference department at K_____ consists of the reference librarian, Miss Elizabeth Harvey, and one professional assistant. One of the more promising young members of the faculty is Richard Hartselle, Assistant Professor of English and Comparative Literature. Professor Hartselle is 34 years old, and has been teaching at K_____ for four years. Two years ago, he completed his doctoral dissertation, a very competent study of the minor novels of Marcel Proust. Professor

25

Hartselle is skilled in Spanish, Russian, French, and German. Although Hartselle is generally respected by members of the faculty and staff, and is idolized by some of the younger students, he is not particularly well liked by his colleagues. He is inclined to be rather cold and reserved, with a peremptory cast to his manner that often makes the simplest request appear to be a command. Although his relations with the library have not been unpleasant, neither could they be described as cordial. On the whole, Hartselle's visits to the library have frequently had the effect of making at least some of the members of the staff feel mildly uncomfortable. It is generally felt that he is a person to be handled as tactfully as possible.

One morning, Professor Hartselle stopped at the reference desk while Miss Harvey was on duty. After an exchange of greetings, Hartselle said, "I wonder if you have a moment, Miss Harvey?"

"Certainly, Dr. Hartselle. I'll be happy to help you if I can."

"The problem is this. I have come across a reference in this article by Kevin Herbert on 'The Theseus theme,' and I'd like to verify it if I can."

Professor Hartselle then produced the January 1960 issue of the *Classical Journal* and pointed to a footnote on page 185.

"You see, this article includes a reference to some of the work of Kazantzakis. You perhaps have seen his sequel to the *Odyssey*. It was published in this country a few years ago."

"Yes, I think we have that in the collection."

"Well I'm not really interested in the *Odyssey* at this point," Hartselle continued, "I'm more concerned with this book, *Tragédies Grecques*. This note states that these plays have never appeared in any language except the French."

Miss Harvey interrupted, "I see that the French edition was published in Monaco in 1953."

Professor Hartselle went on, "Yes. But look at this note."

> There is no indication in the text that these two plays have been published in modern Greek, and to my knowledge they have not appeared in an English version.

Professor Hartselle continued, "What I propose to do is to verify this statement. In other words, I want to find out whether or not this book *has* ever appeared, either in modern Greek or in English. I wonder if you would be good enough to look that up for me?"

"Well, I'll be glad to try to find the information. I'm afraid that it may take a little time."

"Could you telephone me at my office later this afternoon if you've been able to find it?"

The solution to this case involves the verification of the accuracy of the footnote cited above. Your analysis should include a detailed outline of procedures and sources employed to determine whether or not the book in question has indeed ever been published either in English or in modern Greek. Does this case suggest any problems with regard to the establishment of policies limiting the amount of staff time that should be devoted to this kind of assistance to the faculty?

5 Protection of a Student

The University of X_____ is a land-grant college in one of the predominantly rural states of the north central region of the country. Its enrollment of some 7,500 students does not place it in the first rank among publicly supported universities from the point of view of size, and neither is the University of X_____ particularly noted for high quality. In fact, from both points of view, X_____ would best be described as "average" in the hierarchy of state universities at the present time. Its enrollment is chiefly undergraduate, and its strong baccalaureate programs in agriculture and engineering are particularly attractive to students from rural areas. The enrollment in liberal arts programs is somewhat smaller than one might find in a more urban setting. There are also undergraduate programs in education, journalism and nursing. The graduate school, which is not especially large, offers the masters degree in engineering, education and several areas of the liberal arts.

The library of the University of X_____ comprises an adequate, if undistinguished collection numbering some 625,000 items, including government documents, for which the library serves as an official depository. The director, Dr. Hanson, is an elderly man who has been at the university for many years, and whose chief interest lies in regional history and genealogy, in which fields he is considered, at least by local standards, something of an expert. He devotes considerable time to his post as assistant editor of the university's quarterly review, a journal of folklore, anecdotal material, and short articles on the history of the state and region culled largely from the university library's collection of state imprints. Dr. Hanson is charming in a courtly, nineteenth century manner, and is adored by the 35 ladies, of varying ages, on the library staff. He has little time for, or interest in, the

28

day-to-day operations of the library, so that the responsibility for these, over the years, has fallen to a corps of senior members of the staff. Among these is Mrs. Martha Dixon, who is senior reference librarian, and a veteran of some 16 years service in the university library. Mrs. Dixon is a vivacious, pleasant woman, who gives the impression of being vitally interested in the problems of students and faculty, and always seems eager to help in any way she can. Mrs. Dixon is well liked by the whole college community, and new students at the university learn quite early that she is a person who can be very useful in helping them to locate materials and solve problems of study and research.

One afternoon, as Mrs. Dixon was taking her regular turn at the public reference desk, she was approached by a young girl, dressed rather casually, as undergraduates often are, who said, "Where are the books on medicine?"

"Well, they're pretty much scattered through the building. Some are on reserve shelves, others are in the reading rooms, and the older books are mostly in the stacks. Are you having trouble finding a specific book?"

"Not really. It's just that . . ."

"Do you know what particular book you want?"

"I'm afraid I don't. Maybe I should go look again in the catalog."

"Are you looking for a book on a particular subject?" Mrs. Dixon persisted.

"Well, yes, I am."

"Why not look in the catalog under the subject that you're interested in?"

"I've tried that," the girl complained, "but I can't seem to find what I want."

"Can you tell me exactly what subject you want material on? Perhaps you're looking under the wrong thing in the catalog."

"What I really want is to look at some books on children," the student said. "One of my friends told me that I might find some nursing books. Maybe if you could tell me where those are?"

"Well, the books on nursing are up on the next floor," Mrs. Dixon explained, "in the science reading room, but there are so many of them that it might be well for you to use the catalog first. Then you'll know exactly what books you want before you go all the way up there. Are you looking for books on diseases of children, is that it?"

The student was obviously embarrassed, "No. You see . . . Oh, maybe I'll come back another time. I really don't need it today."

"Is this a book for yourself? I mean, just for personal reading, rather than for an assignment."

"Oh, yes!" the girl said.

"Could it be that you want a book on . . . oh, personal hygiene?"

The girl was immensely relieved, "Yes, that's it, I guess."

Convinced that she had at last hit on the right thing, Mrs. Dixon led the student to the card catalog, and located several of the standard, non-technical manuals of sex instruction for her. The student was then shown where these books were located, and, having selected one or two, she left the library.

Mrs. Dixon gave no further thought to the subject, until the following morning when, as she was passing through the science reading room, she noticed the same student, standing in front of the shelves on which reserve books for nursing students were kept. She thought it strange that someone who obviously was not a student nurse should be examining books in that area, and, a short time later, she noticed the same student at the circulation desk, charging out a book. Curiosity got the better of Mrs. Dixon, and, after the student had left the library, she asked the desk attendant to show her the charge card for the book that the student had borrowed. She was somewhat startled to find that the book was John Williams' *Obstetrics* (Appleton, 1961).

Mrs. Dixon recounted the events of the day to her husband at home that evening, and as she finished describing her conversation with the student in question, she said, "You know, George, it just hit me this minute. I'll bet that girl is in trouble. And I wouldn't be surprised if she's planning to try to cover it up by an abortion. That's why she was so nervous and embarrassed when she talked to me yesterday. And that's why she had to come back for more books today, because the books she took yesterday don't deal with that sort of thing."

Her husband agreed that it was certainly possible that the girl was in trouble. The more she thought about the girl and their conversation the more convinced Mrs. Dixon became that what she had mistaken for merely the casual interest of an adolescent girl in sex education materials was, in reality, symptomatic of something potentially far more serious. Mrs. Dixon became increasingly concerned that she might, quite inadvertently, be responsible for the student's having gotten hold of books that could do her great harm. Although she felt a good deal of sympathy and personal responsibility for the girl, she was uncertain as to what course of action, if any, to take.

On the one hand, Mrs. Dixon had no concrete evidence to indicate that the student was planning to do violence to herself, yet all of her suspicions pointed in that direction. Certainly she did not feel that this was a matter for a member of the library staff to attempt to deal with, since it seemed more properly to fall within the province of the Dean of Women. The Dean, however, was notorious on the campus as a heavy-handed, if well-meaning woman, who was utterly lacking in tact, and inclined to be more than a little dictatorial in dealing with students. Mrs. Dixon felt that she ought to report the incident to the Dean, and give her the student's name, which Mrs. Dixon had noted when she examined the circulation record.

To what extent does Mrs. Dixon, as a member of the college staff, have a responsibility for the welfare of individual members of the student body? Should she report this incident to the Dean of Women? What considerations of professional ethics are involved here from the librarian's point of view? If Mrs. Dixon's suspicions should ultimately prove correct, what might the results of reporting the incident to the Dean of Women be from the point of view of the library? Assuming there is no other appropriate university officer who might deal with such matters, are there any alternate courses of action that Mrs. Dixon might consider? How would you evaluate alternatives that might be available to her?

6 A Classic
of Medical Literature

Upland College is a flourishing coeducational institution located near a major industrial and business center in the midwest. The Upland College Library under the direction of Ruth Derby, an energetic and talented woman, has recently begun to emerge from the shadow of many years of neglect, and to assume a place of importance on the Upland campus. During the three years that Miss Derby has held the post of librarian, she has managed to strengthen the staff, to more than double the book budget, and to refurbish the main public areas in the 60 year old college library building.

Over the years, without a particularly conscious effort on anyone's part, the Upland College Library has accumulated, largely by gift, a small but moderately interesting collection of fine bindings, presentation copies, and first editions. Unfortunately, until Miss Derby arrived on the scene, the library had no adequate display facilities for exhibition of such materials. Convinced of the value of occasional exhibitions of rare books and other special materials, Miss Derby managed to obtain administrative approval for the inclusion, as a part of the library's remodelling plan, of an allocation of $11,000 to develop a display area in the main entrance foyer. In justification of this expenditure, Miss Derby pointed out to the president of Upland that exhibits of unusual and interesting books would stimulate student and faculty interest in the library, and, moreover, might be equally useful in attracting gifts from alumni and friends of the college. She emphasized as well the value of such exhibits from a public relations point of view, as they might attract local, and on occasion even national attention in the press.

After the attractive exhibit cases had been selected and installed, the next problem was to find something to put in them, and someone competent to handle exhibits work. Fortunately, Alice Benton, a young professional assistant in the reference department, was found to be particularly talented in these directions, and very enthusiastic about the proposed exhibits program. Under Miss Derby's guidance, Miss Benton quickly set about arranging an exhibit to coincide with the opening of the remodelled sections of the library building.

The initial exhibit, entitled "Uplandiana," was a triumph in every respect. It consisted of historical memorabilia of the college, as well as first editions and presentation copies of books written by faculty and alumni. A capacity crowd attended the opening of the exhibit, where a much publicized young novelist, an Upland alumnus, delivered an address that attracted wide attention in the press.

The president of Upland was equally pleased when he learned, a few days later, that the exhibits area had already begun to attract further gifts to the college. Dr. Howard Shafter, a prominent local physician, had been so impressed by the "Uplandiana" exhibit, that he had decided to present his personal collection of early medical imprints to the college. In due course, the collection arrived at the library, and several months later, after the books had been organized and cataloged, Miss Derby and Miss Benton set about making plans for an exhibit of selected items from the Shafter Collection.

The Shafter Collection included a number of items which, although neither extremely rare nor extremely valuable, were, nevertheless, of genuine interest, such as a sixteenth century edition of Galen, and a first edition of Holmes' *Puerperal Fever* (Boston, 1855). Miss Benton selected some three dozen items to be included in the exhibit, and prepared copy for a small, attractively printed catalog of the collection for public distribution. Once again, a large group of faculty, students and friends of the college were on hand for the opening of the exhibit, including Dr. Shafter, who declared himself highly pleased at the manner in which his gift had been handled.

On the morning following the opening of the Shafter exhibit, Miss Derby had a number of congratulatory notes and telephone calls from faculty and administrative officers of the college. Among the visitors to her office that morning was Dr. Arthur Leland, a senior member of the faculty, and a distinguished microbiologist. After congratulating Miss Derby on the highly successful opening of the Shafter exhibit, Dr. Leland continued as follows:

"You know, Miss Derby, I am something of a collector of medical history myself."

MISS DERBY: "Really? I didn't know that."

DR. LELAND: "Yes, I have a few interesting things. Nothing of the scope of the Shafter Collection, of course. Not on a college professor's salary. By the way, do you know medical literature well, yourself?"

MISS DERBY: "No, I really don't."

DR. LELAND: "Well, then, perhaps I *should* point out that there is one fairly major error in your catalog of the Shafter Collection. I hesitated to say anything, but since you don't know the field yourself, perhaps I might do you a service by mentioning it."

MISS DERBY: "An error?"

DR. LELAND: "Why, yes. You see here on page 2 of your catalog of the Shafter Collection, you say that this edition of Florence Nightingale you have is the first American edition."

Dr. Leland pointed to an entry in the printed catalog, which read:

FLORENCE NIGHTINGALE

Notes on nursing: what it is and what it is not. New York, D. Appleton and Co., 1860. *First American edition,* which appeared in the same year as the original English edition. A true medical classic (Garrison)

DR. LELAND: "There are two things wrong here. First of all, the first English edition of *Notes on Nursing* appeared in 1859, not 1860. Secondly, the first American edition was not the one that you have, but this one."

At that point, Dr. Leland produced from his briefcase a copy of *Notes on Nursing* which may be described bibliographically as follows:

Notes on nursing: what it is and what it is not, by Florence Nightingale, with some account of her life. Boston, William Carter, 5 Water Street, 1860. (Includes biography of Florence Nightingale by Ingleby Scott, pp. i-xii, 1-4. Green binding, stamped in gold, with front cover reproduction of ornament presented to the author by Queen Victoria).

Dr. Leland indicated that the copy described above was his personal one, but that he would be happy to let Miss Derby keep it for a few days if she wished to compare it with the supposed "first edition" in the Shafter Collection. Miss Derby accepted this offer, and said that she would indeed be interested in making such a comparison.

Miss Derby was extremely upset after her conversation with Dr. Leland at the prospect that the Florence Nightingale item was not correctly described in the Shafter Collection catalog. Copies of the catalog had already been sent to a number of libraries, and to several rare book dealers in the area, and the Nightingale item had been described as a "first American edition" in press releases sent both to local newspapers and to various professional library journals. If the copy in the Shafter Collection should indeed prove *not* to be the first American edition, Miss Derby reflected that this could mean considerable embarrassment for the library, for the college, and even for Dr. Shafter. She decided that the first order of business was to determine whether the Shafter copy or the Leland copy of *Notes on Nursing* was the true first American edition.

Miss Derby immediately telephoned Miss Benton, and asked her to remove the Shafter copy of *Notes on Nursing* from the exhibition case, and bring the book to her office. When Miss Benton arrived a few minutes later, Miss Derby repeated the details of her conversation with Dr. Leland. Upon learning that the Shafter copy might not be the first American edition, Miss Benton was equally disturbed. Miss Benton said that she had obtained the information for the catalog description of the Shafter copy of *Notes on Nursing* from a clipping, apparently taken from a dealer's catalog, which had evidently been put inside the book by Dr. Shafter. Further, in order to confirm the accuracy of this clipping, which described the 1860 Appleton edition as the "first American edition," she had consulted the *Catalog of Books Represented by Library of Congress Printed Cards: Supplement . . . August 1, 1942-December 31, 1947*, which lists a 1946 reprint of "a facsimile of the first edition published in 1860 by Appleton-Century" (vol. 27, p. 107). On the basis of this evidence, which was corroborated by Dr. Shafter who had personally reviewed the catalog copy before it was sent to the printers, there had seemed to Miss Benton no question but that the Appleton edition was indeed the first American edition.

The two women made a careful comparison of the Shafter copy of *Notes on Nursing* with the Leland copy, noting the following points of difference in addition to those already mentioned:

1) The Shafter copy, published by Appleton, was bound in blue, with gold letters on the cover, and without the medallion described on the Leland copy published by William Carter.

2) The Shafter copy consisted of 140 pages, consecutively numbered with Arabic numerals, plus four unnumbered pages of advertising matter following p. 140. The Leland copy consisted of pages numbered in the following sequence: iii-iv; i-xii; 1-104, without the advertising matter mentioned above.

3) The Leland copy included the biography of Florence Nightingale by Ingleby Scott, mentioned above, and an index on pp. 5-6, both of which were omitted from the Shafter copy.

4) The Leland copy measured 19.5 cm. in height, the Shafter copy 20 cm.

5) Both copies contained as an "Appendix" a "Note as to the Number of Women Employed as Nurses in Great Britain" consisting of text plus two statistical tables. In the Shafter copy, the tables preceded the text, while in the Leland copy, the text preceded the tables.

6) The type faces used in the Leland copy were quite different from those used in the Shafter copy, so that there seemed no question but that the two books represented different editions of the same work.

Miss Derby asked Miss Benton to undertake immediately such investigations as were necessary in order to determine conclusively which of the two editions of *Notes on Nursing* was, in fact, the true first American edition.

Which of the two editions of *Notes on Nursing* is the "first American edition"? What is the correct date of the first English edition? In determining these facts, it will be important to evaluate carefully the "bibliographical respectability" of the several sources that individually, or collectively, shed light on the problem.

In the light of developments that occurred after the printing of the Shafter catalog, as described in the case, do you feel that the procedures employed by Miss Benton to verify the accuracy of the description of the Shafter copy of *Notes on Nursing* as the first American edition were adequate?

7 Source Material for a Term Paper

The Roger B. Corinth Library, with a collection of 125,000 books and bound periodicals, serves the students and faculty of W_____ College, a co-educational, liberal arts institution with an enrollment of 3,700 undergraduates. W_____, located in a small rural community in one of the middle-Atlantic states, has always been somewhat isolated, since it is away from major lines of transportation and not near any very large city. Perhaps as a consequence of its bucolic setting, the college has, over the 150 years of its existence, been characterized by an atmosphere of relaxation, and an emphasis on the social graces that make it seem, to visitors, almost anachronistic in the modern world. Although it is no longer a church-affiliated school, there is still an emphasis at W_____ on what is described in the college catalog as "the development of Christian virtues among young men and women." The president of W_____ has always been a clergyman, and attendance at twice-weekly, non-denominational chapel services is compulsory for lower classmen.

Members of the college faculty tend to remain in their posts for comparatively long periods of time. Many have spent their entire careers at W_____. Once professorial rank has been achieved, faculty are allowed to do their teaching with a minimum of administrative interference, and there is little of the pressure to "publish or perish" found on most American college campuses today. Most of the members of the faculty are not especially oriented toward research, and although the teaching staff does include one or two productive scholars of national and even international reputation, the emphasis is chiefly on the teaching process.

While the Corinth Library might be considered rather small, in terms of the size of its collection, for a college as large as W_____, it is generally thought quite adequate by students and faculty. Most teaching at W_____ is done along fairly traditional lines, emphasizing the textbook, the lecture and required readings. Thus, the major demand on the library is for reserve books, and except at hours when these become available for circulation, the building is never more than half full.

The library staff is small, numbering seven in addition to the director who also serves as a part-time instructor in the English department. He and two other members of the staff are professionally trained, these latter having the title of "assistant librarian." Although duties and areas of responsibility are rather loosely defined, it is generally understood that Miss Morris, one of the two staff members who has professional training is responsible for cataloging and classification, and that the other trained librarian, Mr. Malvern, takes care of the circulation desk, with student aides handling most of the routines. Such reference service as is required is provided by Mr. Malvern at the circulation desk, since there is not enough of it to warrant setting up and staffing a separate service point.

The reference collection at the Corinth Library comprises approximately 1,000 titles, most of them reasonably up-to-date, with an emphasis on dictionaries, encyclopedias, statistical and biographical sources. Among the major bibliographical reference works available are the *Cumulative Book Index*, the *Reader's Guide to Periodical Literature*, the *International Index*, *PAIS*, *Publisher's Trade List Annual* and its companion volumes, *Biography Index* and *Book Review Digest*, as well as the usual guides to the literature and subject bibliographies. In general, these are little used by students, since few assignments require much in the way of independent investigation.

One afternoon a young man, obviously a student, came up to the circulation desk, where Mr. Malvern was working, and the following conversation ensued:

STUDENT: "Excuse me, could you tell me if the library has the *Debates* of the Province of Saskatchewan?"

MR. MALVERN: "*Debates* of the Province of Saskatchewan? I don't think so. I can't recall ever having seen that. Have you looked in the card catalog?"

STUDENT: "Yes, I looked under 'debates' and under 'Saskatchewan.' It wasn't listed under either of those."

MR. MALVERN: "Those are about the only possibilities, unless perhaps it's treated as a periodical. Do you know if these *Debates* are published in periodical form?"

STUDENT: "I think they come out once a year."

MR. MALVERN: "Just let me check this visible index, to see if we might be receiving it as a periodical. No, it's not listed here either. I'm afraid we don't have it."

STUDENT: "Do you know how I could go about getting it? Could I do it through the library?"

MR. MALVERN: "Possibly. Did you want to look at it in connection with a course?"

STUDENT: "Yes, it's for my term paper on the government in insurance for Dr. Monroe's course in comparative government. He suggested that I look at these Saskatchewan *Debates,* because they have some material on my topic."

MR. MALVERN: "Did he tell you that the library had them?"

STUDENT: "He said he didn't know whether you had them or not."

MR. MALVERN: "You say that you think these *Debates* are published every year?"

STUDENT: "Maybe. I really am not sure. Dr. Monroe didn't say how often they were published but I'm supposed to look at them for 1944."

MR. MALVERN: "Just '1944'? Don't you have a more specific date than that, a month or day?"

STUDENT: "No. That's all Dr. Monroe said, I'm sure. *Debates* of the Province of Saskatchewan for 1944. It's about a law that they passed to sell insurance under government sponsorship."

MR. MALVERN: "Well, as I said before, I'm quite sure that we don't have what you're looking for. No doubt some larger library has it. The problem is, I don't know of any way to find out which library would have it. If it were a regular periodical, I could look it up in the *Union List of Serials,* but that doesn't include most American government documents, let alone Canadian. We don't have any index to the publications of the individual provinces of Canada, either. Anyway, unless you knew the date of the specific issue of the *Debates* that you wanted, we'd have a hard time borrowing it on interlibrary loan from any other library, even if we knew who to ask. Most libraries just won't lend a whole bound volume of a periodical or a serial. The only thing I can think of that we might do is write to the Saskatchewan Provincial Library, or to the National Library of Canada, to see if they could send us a photocopy or a microfilm of the section of the *Debates* that covers this government insurance law. Would you want me to try to do that? You would have to pay the postage and the cost of having a photocopy made, of course, but I don't think it would amount to more than a dollar or two."

STUDENT: "That would be the only way to get hold of it?"

MR. MALVERN: "It's the only way I can think of."

STUDENT: "How long would it take to do that?"

MR. MALVERN: "Oh, probably two or three weeks."

STUDENT: "You mean it would take that long just to get a copy?"

MR. MALVERN: "I expect that it would. Interlibrary loan from a place that far away usually takes at least two weeks."

STUDENT: "I think you'd better forget about it, then. My term paper is due next Monday morning, so it would be too late."

MR. MALVERN: "I see. Well, that's too bad. If you had known that you needed it a little sooner, we might have been able to help you. These things take time you know, and you can't wait until the last minute."

STUDENT: "I guess so."

How would you comment on the manner in which Mr. Malvern handled this reference situation? Given the circumstances of the case, as you know them, do you feel that his response to the problem was an adequate one? Are there alternatives that might have been explored, by way of locating the document in question, that Mr. Malvern has overlooked? Do you feel that his analysis of the problem, as revealed through his comments, was a sound one? Is there any other way in which this student's need for information might have been met?

8 A Proposal to Purchase the Library of Congress Catalogs

Frank Richmond, librarian of R_____ State Teachers College, sat at his desk reading a memorandum that had just come to him from George Wrentham, his reference librarian. The memorandum was in response to an invitation by Mr. Richmond to members of the library's professional staff to submit items to be considered for inclusion in the library's proposed budget for the coming fiscal year. Mr. Wrentham's memorandum read as follows:

TO: Mr. Richmond
FROM: George Wrentham
RE: Budget allocation for reference books

Concerning next year's budget, I should like to recommend, most urgently, that you include an item of $5,000 for the retrospective purchase of a complete set of the printed author and subject catalogs of the Library of Congress, through the most recent issues of the *National Union Catalog*. We should also request $500 for current subscriptions to these catalogs next year.

It is clearly recognized that this recommendation involves a very large sum of money for retrospective purchases, as well as a continuing annual expenditure in the future for current subscriptions to the author and subject catalogs. I know too that the needs of the library are many, and that we face heavy demands for instructional materials from students and faculty. It does seem to me, however, that we can no longer afford to be without these catalogs, which represent the major bibliographical achievement of our century, and must be regarded as vital in any academic library.

Through the catalogs our students and faculty would have direct access to the multi-million volume collections at the Library of Congress, as well as to the current acquisitions of more than six hundred major American and Canadian libraries that participate in the National Union Catalog program. R____ State can never hope to have, nor does it require, a great research library, so that in meeting the specialized book needs of individual students and faculty, we must depend on the resources of other, larger libraries. The printed catalogs of the Library of Congress are the essential key to these resources, and are, therefore, doubly valuable precisely *because* our local resources are so limited.

It should also be noted that these catalogs will be equally useful as we undertake in future years, with the cooperation of the faculty, the long range program for development of the general book collection that you discussed at our last staff meeting. They can be used to supply bibliographical information for book ordering, and should be particularly helpful in cataloging older titles for which printed cards are no longer available.

Finally, there are some sixteen public, special, school and college libraries within a thirty-five mile radius of R____. None of these owns or subscribes to the printed catalogs of the Library of Congress. We are the largest institution in the immediate area, and, as such, I feel we have a responsibility to serve as a center of bibliographical information for our smaller neighbors.

From all of these points of view, I deem the purchase of the printed catalogs of the Library of Congress essential, and hope that it will be possible to provide the necessary funds, as outlined above, next year.

Mr. Richmond read the memorandum through carefully a second time. He was somewhat surprised, indeed even a bit stunned, at its contents, because such a purchase would represent a sizable sum of money in the budget of the R____ College Library. R____ State Teachers College was established some 60 years previously at the turn of the century, as R____ Normal School for the training of elementary and secondary school teachers. It is one of four state-supported institutions for teacher training which, along with an excellent state university some 200 miles from R____, make up the total facilities for public higher education in the state.

Throughout its history, R____ State Teachers College, along with its sister institutions for teacher training, suffered from fiscal neglect by the state legislature. Neither was the school held in particularly high esteem by the general public. A teachers college education was considered "second best" for those who lacked either the financial resources or the intellectual ability to attend a really first-rate college. The maxim "those who can, do; those who can't, teach" seemed the tacit assumption of both the general public and their legislative representatives, so that the meagre funds available for public higher education were channeled largely to the state university. As a result, R_____ became an educational backwater.

Its president, up until five years ago, was an undistinguished political hack who ruled the college like a medieval lord-of-the-manor, while at the same time being careful to avoid any sort of overt action that might attract either public or legislative attention. Under his administration, every effort was made to build up the largest possible student body at the lowest possible cost. Screening of applicants for admission was virtually nonexistent, and any young man or woman who had managed to eke out a high school diploma was welcomed with open arms.

Faculty operated under a set of formulae for grading, devised by the president, the net effect of which was to make it almost impossible to fail any student. Salaries were low, and practically no funds were provided to carry on any sort of reasonable instructional program. Thus, with one or two exceptions, the faculty came to be made up of second and third-rate teachers, many of them holding degrees from R_____ itself or from other institutions of similarly dubious stature—people who taught at R_____ because no other college or university would have them. More than half of the curriculum consisted of courses in methods of teaching, and the size of the faculty in the department of education was larger than the combined total of faculty in all other instructional areas of the college. Some of those holding professorial appointments in education were men and women who, for one reason or another, had themselves been conspicuous failures as elementary and secondary school classroom teachers.

That such a situation could continue for so many years can only be attributed to a completely apathetic attitude on the part of both the legislature and the public. Fortunately, about five years ago, a series of events occurred that brought the college to the attention of the general public in a particularly forceful way. This began with an apparently routine re-accreditation visit by representatives of a national body for the accreditation of teacher-training institutions. At the conclusion of its inspection, the accrediting team announced to the president that re-accreditation would be recommended only on a provisional, three-year basis, and that, at the end of that period, if substantial improvements had not been made in the curriculum, faculty and physical plant of the college, accreditation would be withdrawn. The president re-acted to this news in his characteristic manner by indicating that he had no intention of making any of the recommended changes, that accreditation was "unimportant" to him because the loss of it would not prevent R_____ graduates from being certified to teach in their own state, and that he planned to "ignore the whole business."

Unfortunately for the president, the news of the accreditation situation leaked out to a staff reporter on one of the largest and most powerful metropolitan daily newspapers in the state. This man began a discreet, but thorough investigation of the college, during the course of which he managed not only to obtain complete documentation concerning the pitiful lack of educational facilities at R_____, but also to uncover a particularly scandalous case of flagrantly immoral behavior involving a male member of the college faculty and certain undergraduate women which had long been an open secret on the campus. Over a period of four months, the newspaper had a field day, splashing every sordid detail of the scandal on its editorial pages. At the height of the editorial campaign, a legislative committee was appointed to investigate the situation, and although its report was couched in far more moderate language than the newspaper was using, its conclusions were identical. On the day the committee report was published, the president of R_____, the dean of men, and four of the 50 faculty members holding tenure appointments of professorial rank, resigned *en masse*.

It was against this background of events that Dr. Warren Houston came to R_____ as its new president. Dr. Houston was in his early fifties, held a Ph.D. in classics from a fine eastern university, and had previously served as academic vice president and professor of Greek and Latin at a distinguished small liberal arts college for men, where he had taught for almost twenty years. He had an excellent reputation both as a scholar and as an administrator, and seemed to the governor and the state board of higher education just the sort of person to put the college back on its feet. In four and one-half years, Dr. Houston's accomplishments at R_____ have been impressive. Given a substantial appropriation of money during the first two years of his tenure, and a comparatively free hand in spending it, Dr. Houston was able to strengthen the faculty by bringing in a number of younger men and women with reputable doctorates in the liberal arts and sciences, both as replacements for some faculty members who had resigned and to expand the staff in areas outside of education. It was Dr. Houston's avowed intention to restore a balance between professional courses in methods of teaching and those aimed primarily at the development of subject matter competence. He also planned to initiate a liberal arts curriculum as an alternative to teacher training. His goals were to attain full accreditation both as a teacher-training institution and in the liberal arts.

At the conclusion of his first year in office, the president was able to persuade an aged member of the education faculty, who for reasons of health had been permitted to serve for some ten years as librarian at

R_____ in lieu of a full-time teaching schedule, of the virtues of retirement. Dr. Houston realized the importance of the college library,
both with respect to the immediate problem of accreditation and in
relation to his long term plans for an expanded liberal arts program,
and was anxious to find a well-qualified and dynamic library director.
A few months after the search for a suitable librarian was begun, the
state legislature appropriated three and one-half million dollars for a
combination library-science laboratory building, the first new construction on the campus in almost 50 years, except for federally financed
dormitories. With the prospect of planning a new library building as
an inducement, Dr. Houston was able to persuade Mr. Richmond to
leave his post as associate director of libraries at the state university
and come to R_____.

Although Mr. Richmond had been aware that there were some rather
serious problems at the R_____ College Library, he later confessed to
friends that he was shocked at the magnitude of the task that confronted him. What he found was not a library, in any generally accepted
sense of that term, but merely a collection of old, dirty, unused books,
amounting to about 15,000 volumes, housed in a series of dark, airless
cubicles in the basement of the main college building. The library
"staff" consisted of himself and two elderly women, one of whom ran
the circulation desk while the other handled cataloging. Neither of
these ladies had had any formal training in librarianship, and indeed
both of them were merely high school graduates. For years the library
had kept no records of finances, acquisitions, or use, but it did not require a particularly observant person to realize that for most of the
R_____ community it simply did not exist. On the average, less than
four dozen books a day were borrowed during the school year, and
Richmond found that both faculty and students obtained most of the
books they needed either from public libraries in the area or by buying them.

By questioning his two assistants, Mr. Richmond discovered that the
library had not had a "budget" for more than 25 years. Salaries were
paid from general college funds, and supplies obtained from a central
storeroom as needed. The library had never had a sum of money
allocated to it for the purchase of books. The practice of the former
president had been to inform the heads of academic departments that
"a few hundred dollars" was available for book purchases at the end
of each year, and to divide the sum up among the departments. Each
department head would then proceed to use these funds as he saw fit.
Some departments never bought any books at all with these allocations,
preferring to use the money for other items that they felt were more
important. Those who used the "library money" for books might, or

might not, send their purchases to the library. Many of the books bought in this way lined the walls of faculty offices. And, Mr. Richmond found out, in some years, there had been no money for book purchases at all.

While Mr. Richmond had been merely surprised at the small size of the book collection, he was horrified at its poor quality. He estimated that fully a third of the titles on the shelves should never have been added to the library in the first place, or were so out of date as to be useless for all practical purposes. In this category he counted multiple sets of bound volumes of popular periodicals of thirty or forty years ago, out-dated government documents, ornately bound gift sets of classics of 19th century English literature, and more than one thousand elementary and high school textbooks that had been donated to the library by enterprising publishers' representatives many years before. Of all of the subject areas in the collection, only education and English literature contained even the beginnings of a working library, and even here there was much out-dated material, many poor editions and only a handful of currently useful titles. With these resources, he was expected to serve a student body numbering, at the time of his arrival, some 1,200 undergraduates enrolled in full-time programs leading to the bachelor of science degree in elementary and secondary education, as well as nearly 800 part-time graduate students in late afternoon, Saturday and summer courses leading to the degree of master of education, with specializations in educational administration, guidance and teaching of the handicapped. In addition to providing some sort of reasonable library service to this group on a current basis, Mr. Richmond was further directed by Dr. Houston to develop basic plans for the library portion of the new building, and to proceed to build up a book collection that would be satisfactory to the accrediting agencies with which the college would be involved, and adequate to serve, within ten years, a student body of 2,000 undergraduates, half in liberal arts and half in education, plus 1,200 graduate students.

With the wholehearted cooperation of the president, Mr. Richmond has made real strides in the improvement of library service since his arrival. He has assembled a staff of three professional librarians, including, in addition to Mr. Wrentham, a cataloger and an instructional materials librarian who is also an audio-visual specialist. There is now a supporting clerical staff of three full-time employees plus student aides. The new library building, with seating for 400 and a stack capacity of 125,000 volumes, was opened almost a year and a half ago. Over the past four years, nearly $50,000 has been spent for books, including an allocation during the current fiscal year of $15,000 plus an additional $5,000 in alumni gift funds. The library has grown to

25,000 volumes, even with the removal from the shelves of some 2,000 outdated and worthless items. The total library budget for the current year is approximately $62,000 (including the $5,000 alumni gift) and the rate of current acquisitions is, at present, about 3,700 volumes annually.

Just as substantial improvements have been effected in the library, so have these reflected some dramatic changes in the operation of the college as a whole. The number of full-time faculty holding professorial appointments has been increased to 70, of whom 45 teach in subject areas other than education. Faculty salaries have been increased substantially, at least to the point where the college can begin to compete for competent younger people, although rates of compensation are still comparatively poor at the higher levels and some of the best teachers still leave after a few years for more attractive positions elsewhere.

Although the student body has grown to 1,500 undergraduates and nearly 1,000 graduate students, there has, at the same time, been a gradual stiffening of academic standards. Some seventy-five percent of the undergraduates are still working toward the bachelor of science degree in education, although the curriculum in this area has been revamped, so that more than two-thirds of the total work is done in the liberal arts and sciences, with the remaining third in professional courses. The rest of the undergraduates are enrolled in a new liberal arts program which, at the present time, offers majors in eleven fields, including chemistry, biology, mathematics, history, sociology, government, English literature, French, Spanish, psychology and American civilization.

President Houston has been very successful in raising funds, and in obtaining legislative support for the new programs. The current budget of the college for educational and general expenses, exclusive of the operation of the dormitories and dining halls, is approximately $1,000,-000 (as contrasted with $590,000 four years ago). He has worked hard to publicize new activities and to create a more favorable public image for the college. Overall, his administration has been a successful one, although he has made enemies both among the faculty and in certain alumni circles. There is still a good deal of deadwood on the faculty, and it is anticipated that this will continue to be the case for many years to come. Of late, President Houston has encountered fairly substantial resistance in influential quarters of the legislature in his efforts to obtain even larger appropriations for current operating expenses. His most recent proposal, calling for a bond issue to construct a combination classroom and student union building, was defeated by a substantial margin. He has, however, managed to have the teacher training program reaccredited, and it is his expectation to seek liberal arts accreditation three years hence.

After he had studied Mr. Wrentham's memorandum concerning the proposed purchase of the Library of Congress catalogs for a few days, Mr. Richmond scheduled a conference with his reference librarian. When the latter arrived in his office on the appointed morning, the conversation between the two men was as follows:

MR. RICHMOND: "George, I suspect that you know why I asked you to stop by this morning."

MR. WRENTHAM: "To tell you the truth, Frank, I rather imagined that you might want to discuss my recommendation about the LC catalogs."

MR. RICHMOND: "Yes, that's the chief thing that I wanted to talk with you about, but I would like to frame this discussion in a somewhat larger context. Let me see, you've been with us just over a year now, isn't that right?"

MR. WRENTHAM: "Fifteen months, to be exact."

MR. RICHMOND: "Right! Well, I think that this might be an appropriate point for us to sort of review the things that you have been doing, and to see how these will fit into the general scheme in the future. While some of these things are not specifically related to this recommendation of yours about the Library of Congress catalogs, I must say that it *was* your memo that stimulated me to think along these lines. Let me begin by saying that you were given a difficult assignment here, and that I think you have done a first-rate job. I couldn't be happier with your work, and I hope that you have been reasonably happy here as well. Now I hope you know that one of the things I have tried to do is to keep you fully informed about such things as budget, curriculum planning and my own relationship with the president as this affects the library. I think I am safe in saying that you know just about as much about the frame of reference within which I have to work as I do, wouldn't you agree?"

MR. WRENTHAM: "Yes, you've been very open with me in that respect, and I appreciate it."

MR. RICHMOND: "When you came here, I told you that your responsibilities would be varied, but that they would fall basically in four areas: first, to assume general supervisory responsibility for the whole public service operation of the library with the exception of the instructional materials center; second, to establish and man a point of professional reference service within the library; third, to develop, by working with the faculty, a meaningful program of instruction in the use of the library for students; and fourth, as a supplement to what the faculty can contribute in this respect, to begin a systematic evaluation of the book collection. Now, I'd like to ask you, as a kind of preface to our discussion of this recommendation of yours, where you think you stand right now in each of these four areas?"

MR. WRENTHAM: "Well, on the first, I would say things are quite well in hand. This is basically a matter of keeping an eye on the circulation desk and Miss Stickney has been at that job for so many years that she really requires very little of anyone's time.

"As for the reference desk, I am reasonably well-satisfied that we have made a good start, although, as you know, it takes time to get students and faculty into the habit of using a service when that service has never existed in the past. I think that this is largely a matter of availability on my part, so that most of my working day has gone into manning the desk.

"On the instructional end, I've devoted a great deal of effort to this this year, but it's terribly difficult to crack most of the people on the faculty. Aside from the library handbook, and the freshmen tours, we've made very little progress, and I would expect that it will take a lot more hard work on my part next year.

"As for the evaluation of the collection and the whole matter of an acquisitions program, I've done practically nothing on this except to look over the reference collection. For one thing, I haven't had time, and for another it seemed to me that a decent reference collection, with adequate bibliographic sources, is just fundamental to any activity of this kind. To my way of thinking, until we have the LC catalogs and some other basic sources, we can't even begin to do much about the general collection. Also, I wanted to talk over the whole matter of acquisitions with you to see just what you had in mind, and what my role would be *vis-a-vis* the faculty."

MR. RICHMOND: "I think that's a very modest assessment of your accomplishments in the past year and a half, George, but let's assume for a moment that it's a fair one. Now, let me sketch out what I had in mind in the way of an acquisitions program for the future. I am aiming towards a book collection of about 100,000 currently useful items. I think that is a reasonable and adequate ten-year goal in terms of our instructional programs. This would mean adding about 70,000 volumes to the collection in the next ten years. This year we will add about 3,700 volumes, and next year I'd like to make that figure 5,000. Allowing for gifts and bound volumes of serials, that suggests a book budget of about $25,000. I hope that $5,000 of that can be obtained from alumni again next year, so that $20,000 would come from state funds.

"About 30 percent of the total book budget goes every year, as you know, to meet our subscription and standing order obligations.

That leaves us $17,500 to play around with, of which we'll need at least $10,000 to buy items requested by the faculty, mostly current titles, duplicate copies for reserve book shelves, and so on. My intention had been to set aside $5,000 to begin making substantial additions to the general book collection in the form of major sets, runs of bound and microfilmed periodicals and the like. As you know, the various departments have been at work all year building up want lists for a retrospective buying program which I have promised we'll start next year. My plan had been to give you the remaining $2,500 to begin a similar buying program for the general reference collection. Does this sound reasonable to you?"

MR. WRENTHAM: "Well, you've had a lot more experience with this sort of thing than I have, and I must admit it does sound reasonable. The only thing that disappoints me is, what you have said seems to rule out the LC catalogs next year."

MR. RICHMOND: "Precisely. Actually, I'm afraid it's even worse than that, at least from the point of view of your recommendation. You know, as well as I do, that we seem to have reached a kind of plateau as far as financing the college is concerned. President Houston has made it pretty clear that the day of huge budget increases is just about over, and that our appropriations from the state can be expected to level off for the next few years.

"Now, the other factor involved in all of this discussion of book budget is staff. Our staff is more than 100% larger today than it was just four years ago. I think it's going to be a while before I can reasonably ask for even one more person. This too suggests a leveling off of the book budget, because I don't see any point in our getting into a situation where our staff is too small to process the number of books that we're buying. I think that for at least the next four or five years we'll have to work with a fairly stable book budget of around $25,000 a year, divided up about along the lines that I've indicated. So, without some fairly major changes in my basic plan of budget allocation, I just don't see where the $5,000 that you're asking for is going to come from, do you?"

MR. WRENTHAM: "Well, I see two ways in which we could do this—actually, three ways. First, you could defer the start of the general retrospective buying program for one more year, and use the $5,000 to buy the LC catalogs. If that's impractical, you could use $2,500 of the retrospective purchase money, over the next two years. The third possibility would be for me to do the same thing with my reference book budget for the next two years."

MR. RICHMOND: "If we chose the last alternative, this would mean that you wouldn't be able to buy any other reference books at all until three years from now. Would you be willing to do that?"

MR. WRENTHAM: "Yes, if necessary I would."

MR. RICHMOND: "Do you have a pretty clear notion at this point of what our total needs for reference books are going to be?"

MR. WRENTHAM: "Not in terms of specific titles, in any complete way. I haven't gotten to that point yet. But I can tell you we literally need *everything*. I think an adequate reference collection for a college this size would be about 1,500 titles, without going beyond anything that I consider really basic. Offhand, I would guess that we might have three or four hundred of these titles now."

MR. RICHMOND: "You used the word 'guess.' Do you mean that you're not certain what we do have in the collection right now?"

MR. WRENTHAM: "I certainly know what we don't have. We don't have any up-to-date encyclopedias, we don't have any of the specialized periodical indexes except *Education Index*, we don't have a foreign language dictionary that was published later than 1900, we don't have *Chemical Abstracts*, we don't have *PAIS* or *Vertical File Index*—shall I go on?"

MR. RICHMOND: "George, you don't have to. I get the point. In fact, I'm painfully aware of just these limitations that you speak of, and this is the real reason that your recommendation on the Library of Congress catalogs knocked me for a bit of a loop. Putting aside the question of finances for a moment, and even assuming that this could be gotten around in one of the ways that you suggest, what *really* bothers me about your recommendation is the appropriateness of such a purchase for a library like ours. Don't you feel, in all honesty, that these very items you've just spoken of, and I could add two dozen more equally basic things right off the top of my head, just *must* take precedence in any purchasing that we do?

"I can't see how we could *consider* buying the LC catalogs at this stage of the game, and frankly, I'm not at all sure that I would ever consider them an appropriate purchase for a library the kind and size of ours. Now please understand, I'm not turning you down, I'm really asking a question of you—I'm asking for your best judgment as our reference specialist. In the light of what we've just been saying, do you still want to let your original recommendation that we buy these stand?"

Mr. Wrentham thought for a few moments before replying to Mr. Richmond's last question, then he said: "Yes, Frank, I do want to let it stand. I've indicated my reasons in my memo, and I don't mean to repeat them here. We *do* have a limited book collection, and we will always have one. I think that this imposes a special obligation on us to build up a particularly strong bibliographic reference collection. When we have to send a student or a faculty member to another library, or when we have to borrow something on interlibrary loan, I think we must never be in the position where we're asking another library to do bibliographical reference work for us.

"This means that we've got to be able to translate the vague requests that students and faculty bring to us into specific authors and titles that we can ask for with a minimum of effort on the part of the lending library. Without a decent working collection of bibliographical reference sources, we're going to be continually asking other libraries to do this kind of reference work for us, in addition to asking them to lend us the books and journals that are needed here. The only other thing that I would add is this. We're very concerned about accreditation. I'm told that accrediting teams will often check library holdings against standard lists. Well, the LC catalogs appear on *every* standard list of recommended reference books for college libraries that I've ever seen."

MR. RICHMOND: "Those are good points, George, I must admit. Tell me, have you discussed the possibility of our buying the LC catalogs with any members of the faculty?"

MR. WRENTHAM: "No, I haven't."

MR. RICHMOND: "Let me ask you this. Has any member of the faculty ever asked for them, or suggested that we buy them?"

MR. WRENTHAM: "No."

MR. RICHMOND: "George, in the time that you've been here, how often would you say that you have had a reference question from a student or a member of the faculty that you were not able to answer because we don't own the LC catalogs?"

MR. WRENTHAM: "That's kind of a hard question to answer, Frank. I've never kept a record of them. Perhaps I should have."

MR. RICHMOND: "Well, just off the top of your head. How often? Once a week?"

MR. WRENTHAM: "No, not that often, I guess. Why, I don't even get a real reference question once a week, some weeks. Just simple directional questions as to where things are, or how to use the card catalog."

MR. RICHMOND: "Well, once a month?"

MR. WRENTHAM: "Yes, I think that's closer to it. Once or twice a month, I could have used the LC catalogs."

MR. RICHMOND: "Let's say twice a month, just to be fair. Then what it comes down to is you're asking me to spend over $5,000 to answer 30 reference questions. If my mathematics is correct, that's almost $200 per question. I would call that pretty expensive reference service, wouldn't you?"

MR. WRENTHAM: "With all due respect, Frank, I don't think that's really fair. In the first place, what we're discussing here is practically a lifetime investment for this library. These catalogs aren't going out of date—they're going to be useful to us, if we buy them, for many, many years to come. And, I think too that we can reasonably expect the demand for reference service to grow in the future, as people here become accustomed to using it. I can't resist adding, on that score, that the surest way to make this happen is for us to be in a position to provide satisfactory service each and every time we are given the opportunity. Nothing attracts customers like a satisfied customer."

MR. RICHMOND: "George, this has been a very helpful discussion for me. I do see your point of view on this, and I hope that you, in turn, see some of the difficulties that I will have to face, if I decide to approve your recommendation and buy the catalogs. I'm not going to give you an answer on this today, because I want to give the whole business some more thought. There is one thing that you could do, if you would, that would be very helpful to me."

MR. WRENTHAM: "Certainly, Frank. What is it?"

MR. RICHMOND: "Could you let me have a list, just in rough form, of the bibliographical portion of the existing reference collection, as distinguished from the fact-finding part. Would this be a terribly time-consuming job for you?"

MR. WRENTHAM: "Not in the least. We have so little material of this kind that it would be very simple. I'll see that you have it this afternoon."

Mr. Wrentham was as good as his word, and the list was on Mr. Richmond's desk the same afternoon. (It is reproduced as *Appendix I* of this case study.) During the next few days, Mr. Richmond tried to determine, in a very informal way, how much progress had been made by the various instructional departments of the college in developing retrospective want lists. He concluded from this investigation that he could expect to receive, some six weeks hence on the day these lists were to be turned in to the library, recommendations for purchases amounting to at least $30,000.

In the light of all that you know about R_____ State Teachers College and its library, would you, had you been in Mr. Wrentham's place, have recommended the purchase of the Library of Congress catalogs at this time, as he did? How do you evaluate the arguments presented by Mr. Wrentham in favor of the purchase both in his memorandum and in his subsequent conversation with Mr. Richmond? Which, if any, of Mr. Wrentham's suggestions concerning methods of financing the purchase of the catalogs do you consider sound? How would you answer Mr. Richmond's questions concerning the *appropriateness* of the LC catalogs for a library like R_____'s, either at the present time or at any future time? What factors will Mr. Richmond have to take into consideration in reaching a decision with regard to Mr. Wrentham's recommendation? If a decision should be made to purchase the catalogs, what would you expect the reaction of the college faculty to be? How might Dr. Houston be expected to react to the inclusion of such an item in Mr. Richmond's proposed budget for next year? If you were in Mr. Richmond's position, would you approve Mr. Wrentham's recommendation, and if so, how would you implement your decision?

■ APPENDIX I

A List of Bibliographical Reference Sources Currently in the R—— State Teachers College Library

A.L.A. *Catalog*, 1926, and Supplements, 1-4.
A.L.A. *Catalog*, 1904-1911.
Bibliographic Index, 1956-1960.
Cumulative Book Index, 1928—date.
McKerrow. *An Introduction to Bibliography*. 1927.
The United States Catalog. 4th ed. 1928.
American Library Association. *Inexpensive Books for Boys and Girls*. 3rd ed. 1952.
American Library Association. *A Basic Book Collection for Junior High Schools*. 1950.
Bertalan. *Books for Junior Colleges*. 1954.
Carnegie Corporation. *A List of Books for Junior College Libraries*. 1937.
Shaw. *A List of Books for College Libraries*. 1931, and 1st. *Suppl.*
Colburn. *Books and Library Reading for Pupils in the Intermediate Grades*. 1942.
Graham. *Bookman's Manual*. 7th ed., 1954.

Great Books of the Western World. 1952.
Hirshberg. *Subject Guide to Reference Books*. 1942.
Iowa University. *A Guide to Literature for Character Training*. 1928-1930.
American Library Association. *A Basic Book Collection for Elementary Grades*. 1951.
Junior Reviews' Catalog of the Best Books for Children. 1954.
Logasa. *Historical Fiction*. 5th ed. 1951.
Mahony. *Five Years of Children's Books*. 1936.
Mahony. *Realms of Gold in Children's Books*. 1929.
Mudge. *New Guide to Reference Books*. 1923.
Periodicals for Small and Medium Sized Libraries. 1948.
Rue. *Subject Index to Books for Intermediate Grades*. 1950.
Rue. *Subject Index to Readers*. 1938.
Rue. *Subject Index to Books for Primary Grades*. 1943.
Shores. *Basic Reference Sources*. 1954.

Shores. *Basic Reference Books.* 1939.
Strang. *Gateways to Readable Books.* 1944.
Subscription Books Bulletin.
Wilson. *Children's Catalog,* 1956. plus *Supplements,* 1957-1960.
Wilson. *Fiction Catalog.* 1941. *Supplements,* 1942-1949.
Wilson. *Standard Catalog for Public Libraries.* 4th ed. and *Supplements.*
Winchell. *Guide to Reference Books.* 7th ed.
Biography Index, 1946—date.
Book Review Digest, 1937—date.
The New York Times Index, 1945.
International Index to Periodicals, 1960 —date.
Reader's Guide to Periodical Literature, 1900—date.
Education Index, 1930—date.
National Geographic Magazine Cumulated Index, 1899-1946.
Lyle. *Classified List of Periodicals for the College Library,* 1948.
Ulrich's Periodicals Directory. 1953.
Monthly Catalog of U.S. Government Publications, 1951—date.
Index to Publications of the U.S. Department of Agriculture, 1926-1930, 1931-1935.
Hirshberg. *Subject Guide to U.S. Government Publications.* 1947.
Buros. *Mental Measurements Yearbook* (3rd, 4th and 5th)
Haywood. *A Bibliography of North American Folklore and Folksong.*
Minneapolis Public Library. *An Index to Folk Dances and Singing Games.*

American Library Association. *Subject Index to Children's Plays.* 1940.
Firkins. *Index to Plays.*
Hiler. *Bibliography of Costume.* 1939.
Ottemiller. *Index to Plays in Collections.* 1957.
Ottemiller. *Index to Plays in Collections.* 1943.
Sutton. *Speech Index.*
Baldensperger. *Bibliography of Comparative Literature.* 1960.
Brewton. *Index to Children's Poetry.* 1942.
Bruncken. *Subject Index to Poetry.* 1940.
Eastman. *Index to Fairy Tales, Myths and Legends.* 1926. Supplement. 1937.
Essay and General Literature Index. 1948—date.
Firkins. *Index to Short Stories.* 2nd ed. 1923.
Granger. *Index to Poetry.* 4th ed. 1953.
Lenrow. *Reader's Guide to Prose Fiction.* 1940.
Short Story Index. 1953—date.
The Cambridge Bibliography of English Literature.
Coan. *America in Fiction.* 3rd ed. 1949.
Griffith. *A Bibliography of Chaucer.* 1926.
Slocum. *A Bibliography of James Joyce.* 1953.
Forrester. *Occupational Literature.* 1954.
A Guide to Historical Literature. 1931.
Harvard Guide to American History. 1954.

9 Right to Work Laws

The firm of V_____ Laboratories is engaged chiefly in conducting research on a contract basis for the federal government and private industry. The company employs more than 400 scientists, as well as a large supporting staff of engineers, technicians, and other workers. At any given time, V_____ Laboratories is likely to have 50 or more projects under way, representing a variety of original investigations. While the firm is chiefly known for its work in the field of light metals, it has capabilities in several other areas as well.

V_____ Laboratories maintains operations at five different locations in the United States, although its headquarters are on the west coast. In addition to the executive offices, the west coast installation is the home of the light metals and alloys laboratory with a staff of nearly 300 scientific and technical people. As might be expected in a firm oriented chiefly toward research, V_____ Laboratories provides a very complete research library at its home office. Conveniently located in the laboratory building, it is spacious, attractive and well organized, and contains approximately 25,000 items related to the various fields in which the company has interest. The collection includes some 4,000 books, and nearly 12,000 bound and microfilmed volumes of technical journals in metallurgy and related subjects. The remainder of the library consists largely of technical reports, including those produced by the firm itself, agencies of the federal government, and private industry.

The research library is staffed by a librarian, Judith Ferriday, and two clerical assistants. Miss Ferriday is a recent graduate of a library school, and also holds a baccalaureate degree in chemistry. At the time the events in this case occurred, she had been employed by the firm for just three weeks. One morning, she received a telephone call from a Miss Parsons, who indicated that she was a secretary in the office of

Robert Ware, the company's president. After Miss Parsons had introduced herself, the telephone conversation continued as follows:

MISS PARSONS: "Miss Ferriday, I'm calling for Mr. Ware. He's scheduled to participate in a panel discussion on Friday of this week in Chicago on labor-management relations. He's flying there Thursday evening, day after tomorrow, and he wondered if you might be able to get some material for him."

MISS FERRIDAY: "I'll certainly be happy to try. What sort of material does he need?"

MISS PARSONS: "Just a minute, I have it written down, if I can find my note pad. Oh yes, here it is. The panel is on the open shop law and the right to work. Does that mean anything to you?"

MISS FERRIDAY: "Yes, vaguely. That is, I remember it from college. But, I'm afraid it doesn't have much to do with the contents of the library here. If Mr. Ware needs material on that, I suppose that I'd have to go to another library to find it."

MISS PARSONS: "Well, you would know best about that. You understand, I'm just delivering the message for Mr. Ware."

MISS FERRIDAY: "Did he want information about some specific aspect of right-to-work laws?"

MISS PARSONS: "Yes. He would like to know what the effect of open shop laws has been on wages in those states where they exist. I suppose he means whether wages have gone up or down as a result of these laws being in force."

MISS FERRIDAY: "Was there anything else in the way of specific information?"

MISS PARSONS: "Not according to my notes. He said that he'd be grateful for any sort of general background material that you might be able to find."

MISS FERRIDAY: "Does he want this in the form of a report from me, or does he just want me to gather together some articles and things for him to read, himself?"

MISS PARSONS: "He didn't say."

MISS FERRIDAY: "I'll do my best. Was there anything else?"

MISS PARSONS: "Yes. Mr. Ware asked me to tell you that he's sorry to burden you with this, because he knows you must be busy getting acquainted with the library. He also said to tell you that he hopes to stop by and meet you when he returns from the Chicago trip."

MISS FERRIDAY: "Well, that's very nice of him. You'll need to have the material day after tomorrow?"

MISS PARSONS: "Yes, before three, if you can. If you'll just call me when it's ready, I'll send a messenger down to pick it up."

Miss Ferriday was somewhat puzzled as to how to handle Mr. Ware's request for information in the most expeditious way. Aside from a dictionary, a general encyclopedia and a copy of *Who's Who in America,* the research library contained no reference materials except for those dealing with the specialized field of metallurgy. She therefore assumed that she would have to go elsewhere, presumably to the public library, to locate the things she needed. Since she did not know exactly what was available on the subject of right-to-work laws, she could hardly avoid making a personal trip to the library in order to locate the appropriate materials. Although she knew that the local public library was an excellent one, and presumably would have adequate material on the subject, she was not particularly pleased at having to make a trip there at this point. Because there had been a hiatus between her predecessor's departure and her arrival, and because she was still having a bit of difficulty in finding her way around the library, Miss Ferriday had fallen somewhat behind in her work. She had two literature searches under way at the moment, neither of which had been completed, and one of these had been promised for the very day on which the report for Mr. Ware was now due.

The solution to this problem consists of locating source materials on the subject of right-to-work laws and preparing a report that will serve as an adequate response to Mr. Ware's request for information. In what form would you present this material? Consideration should be given, in the development of the analysis, to the fact that Miss Ferriday has only a limited amount of time in which to work, and at least one other major obligation that requires her attention. What sort of priority ought to be given to this request under these circumstances?

10 A Memorial Plaque

Mrs. Jane Rustin is librarian of D_____ Junior High School. Located in a suburban community near a large eastern city, D_____ Junior High School has an enrollment of 700 students in grades seven, eight and nine. The librarian has no salaried assistants, although she has organized a group of students to serve as "library aides" on a voluntary basis. One morning recently, John Herrin, an eighth grader, was helping Mrs. Rustin to shelve books. When the work had been completed, the boy said, "Mrs. Rustin, could I ask you something?"

"Certainly, John. What is it?"

"Well, you know, my father has a lot of slides that he took last summer when he and my mother were in Europe."

"Oh, yes. I remember you told me about their trip."

"You see, he took all these pictures, and had them made up into slides. He has a tape recorder too, and he's recording an explanation of each picture—what it is, you know," John continued. "Well, he was working on it last night, and he said that he'd like to have a slide with a map of Paris on it. If he had a map of Paris, one that's in color, he could take a picture of that and show it with his slides. I was telling him about the library here and all the books, and he said to ask you if you knew where he could borrow a map of Paris, just to take a picture of it."

"Well, now, that shouldn't be too hard to find, John. Let me think for a minute."

"Mrs. Rustin, I have to go back to my home room in a minute. While you're thinking, could I ask you one other question? My father has some pictures of the house in Paris where John Paul Jones died. One picture shows a plaque—my father says it's on the second floor of the

59

house. He wanted me to ask you if there's any way of finding out who put that plaque there. He was showing his slides to some people the other night, and someone asked him. He doesn't know who put it there, but I thought maybe you could tell me who did. Would it be in some encyclopedia, or something?"

"Do you know what the plaque says?"

"I've got it written down. My father's got a great picture of it, and we copied it off that. But I can't read it, because it's in French."

"Can your father read French?"

"I don't think so. Not very good. Anyway, here's what it says."

At this point, John produced a slip of paper on which the following had been carefully printed:

John Paul Jones, premer amiral de la Marine des Etats-Uni et un des heroes de la Guerre de Independence Americaine, est mort dans cette maison le 18 Julliet 1792.

Mrs. Rustin promised to think about where a map of Paris, from which a slide could be made, and the source of the memorial plaque to John Paul Jones might be located. The boy said that he would stop at the library after school, before going home, in the hope that she could tell him how his father might go about finding the information.

The D_____ Junior High School library consists of about 3000 books, with some 200 volumes on the reference shelves. These include the *Abridged Readers' Guide, Current Biography. Biography Index,* the *New Century Cyclopedia of Names,* the *Dictionary of American Biography,* a recent edition of *Goode's World Atlas,* Adams' *Atlas of American History,* several dictionaries, recent printings of *Collier's Encyclopedia* and the *World Book Encyclopedia,* an older *Britannica,* a full set of *Collier's Annual,* the *World Almanac, Statistical Abstract,* and a variety of subject handbooks and literary sourcebooks. About ten percent of the annual book budget of $1,200 is used for the purchase of reference books, and an equal amount goes to maintain current subscriptions to 35 periodicals. There is also a small pamphlet collection, consisting mostly of free material, which fills four large file drawers. The community of 15,000 in which the school is located has a small, rather poorly supported public library.

How would you suggest that Mrs. Rustin respond to the questions that John Herrin has raised? What sources would be likely to produce the two things that John's father is seeking? To what extent should Mrs. Rustin assist in locating this information? Can you locate a map of Paris that would be satisfactory for the purpose for which it is needed as described in the case? Can you find out who was responsible for the memorial plaque to John Paul Jones described in the case? Can these questions be answered from resources that either are known to be available, or might reasonably be expected to be available, in the community where the D_____ Junior High School is located?

11 Improper Use of
Reference Materials

The town of L_____ is an exclusive residential suburb of a large eastern city. L_____ has a population of 21,000, and is a community of fine homes, most of which are in the $30,000 to $40,000 price range. Nearly 60 percent of the employed residents occupy positions at professional, technical or managerial levels. Both average income and educational level are high. By any standards, L_____ is a wealthy community. Its citizens are accustomed to municipal services of superior quality, and have shown an unusual willingness to provide public funds in sufficient amounts to make this possible. The town was one of the first to adopt stringent zoning regulations, and these have served, in turn, to prevent an inordinate increase in the population, in spite of the post-war exodus to the suburbs which has troubled neighboring communities. School population, for example, has increased only slightly in L_____ during the past ten years, and, although the town has built two new schools during this period, this stemmed from a desire to replace older buildings rather than from any shortage of classroom facilities.

The town's public schools are reputed to be among the finest in the state, if not in the nation. The people of L_____ have repeatedly made it clear that they will settle for nothing but the best when it comes to education for their children. The school system is handsomely financed, and salary scales for teachers are among the highest in the country. The buildings are modern and attractive, and provide virtually every facility known to modern education. Close ties are maintained with neighboring universities and colleges, and the school administrators enthusiastically foster and encourage new and experimental programs in education. Faculty standards are high throughout the L_____ schools, and mediocre teachers do not remain long on the staff.

The L_____ Public Library has also benefited from this interest in the schools, and its director, Mr. Peabody, has succeeded in creating a highly favorable climate of public opinion toward the library as part of the total educational resources of the community. Although there are school libraries at every level throughout the system, the community has accepted the thesis that a strong public library is also essential to provide a full range of educational opportunities for its children.

Mr. Peabody frankly admits that he has for several years pursued a policy of "riding the coat tails of the Superintendent of Schools" in seeking funds for the library. The success of this approach is reflected in the fact that the L_____ Public Library is housed in a fine, modern building, and that the quality of the book collection is equally high. The library operated last year on a budget of $116,000, thus giving it a per capita support slightly in excess of $5.50. The library staff numbers 16, of whom seven are professionally trained. Two librarians are assigned to provide reference and advisory service to young people and adults at a continuously staffed point of professional service in the reference room. One of these, Mr. Webster, has the title of Reference Librarian.

One afternoon, as Mr. Webster was seated at the reference desk, a young man approached him, carrying a volume of the *Book Review Digest,* and the following conversation ensued:

"Are you the librarian here?"

"Yes, I'm the Reference Librarian. My name is Webster."

"Mr. Webster, I'm Dick Eustis. I'm on the faculty at the high school."

"Well, it's a pleasure to meet you, Mr. Eustis. I'm really surprised that we haven't met before. Have you been in L_____ long?"

"This is my first year here, and, actually, my first visit to your library as well. I'm here today, I'm afraid, on rather an unpleasant errand. One of my students . . . I teach eleventh grade English . . . has been dishonest in writing a book report, and this dishonesty involves the library."

"Why, I'm very surprised to hear that, and I'm not certain that I quite understand."

"Let me explain, Mr. Webster. I'm sure that neither you nor anyone else here would intentionally help a student to cheat. I prefer to think that this represents what might be called a misguided attempt to be helpful."

"Misguided?"

"Yes. I asked one of my classes to write a report on one of Steinbeck's novels, and to include an evaluation of Steinbeck's social philosophy. I made it quite clear that this was to be their *personal* evaluation."

"Yes?"

"What happened was this. One of the boys got hold of this book digest, here, apparently at your suggestion, and simply copied quotations from reviews of Steinbeck's books. His classmates felt that these ideas were so much better than what they'd been able to come up with on their own that they in turn copied the first student's work. As a result, the whole assignment was a complete failure as far as I was concerned."

"I'm sorry to learn about this, Mr. Eustis. I do recall a boy asking for help in finding information about Steinbeck's social thought, and I believe I did suggest looking at reviews of *The Grapes of Wrath*. Of course, I had no idea that they were not supposed to use sources for the assignment."

"Well, that's all water over the dam as far as I'm concerned. I'm here today to find out what you intend to do to prevent any recurrence of this kind of incident."

"Mr. Eustis, we have always had a policy here of cooperating with the schools one hundred percent."

"Fine. First, I'd prefer that, in the future, you give no assistance of any kind to any of my students. Also, I've been looking over the books in this room, and I must say that I'm rather astonished to find that you not only have this *Book Review Digest* in plain sight, but several other books that seem to give plot summaries as well. Are these always left out in the open this way?"

"Yes. The whole library is an open shelf collection."

"Well, I'd like you to put this *Book Review Digest* and some of the others in some closed area where my students won't be using them to write book reports."

"Why, I couldn't do anything like that. These books are needed for reference purposes. They're used every day. We have to keep them here where people can get at them."

"I'm sorry, but I must insist that these books be removed from this room today."

"Mr. Eustis, I've listened to about all that I intend to listen to on this subject. I don't like your attitude, or your accusations, and I certainly don't like your coming in here, trying to turn this library upside down."

"Do you mean that you will go right on encouraging students to use these books?"

"I didn't say that."

"You didn't have to. I can tell you that I intend to see that something is done about this. There are plenty of people in this town who are interested in cooperating with teachers, even if you're not."

Mr. Webster was upset after his rather unpleasant conversation with Mr. Eustis, and somewhat uncertain about what to do next. He recounted the incident to his assistant, Miss Paterson, when she arrived to take desk duty that evening. The next morning, when Mr. Webster returned to the library, he found the following note on his desk from Miss Paterson:

"Thought that you would like to know that after you left yesterday, your friend Mr. Eustis came in again with some people who I think I recognized as 'PTA.' He showed them *Book Review Digest* and some other books. Hope this doesn't mean more trouble."

Mr. Webster immediately went to Mr. Peabody's office, and recounted to him all the events of the previous day. When he had finished, Mr. Peabody said, "Arthur, this has all the makings of a nasty little tempest in a teapot, especially if the PTA is involved. That's one group that I wouldn't like to tangle with. Also, I've got to admit that your Mr. Eustis has some fairly strong arguments."

"You're right, George, of course. I must say that I got steamed up yesterday, and perhaps I wasn't thinking too clearly. I can understand that he might be upset under the circumstances."

"I gather, though, that you don't want to take the books in question off the open shelves."

"Let's say that I'm not prepared to at this point. Naturally, if you wish it, I'll take them off."

"Arthur, you know that I'll back you to the limit on anything like this, as long as you're able to convince me that you're right. By all means, leave the books where they are for the moment. By the way, have we had any other complaints like this from teachers?"

"Not that I know of."

"How many other people teach English at the high school?"

"Oh, five or six, I suppose."

"Well, what do you suggest we do? Are you absolutely certain that you're right about this, and that these books should be kept on the open shelves?"

"To be honest with you George, I'm not. I think I'm right, but I see Eustis' point too."

"If my guess is correct, either Mr. Eustis, or the PTA people, or both will be wanting to see me about this, probably today. Suppose I do this. I'll try to put them off until tomorrow afternoon, if I can. In the meantime, you think it over and make your decision. Let's you and I have lunch together tomorrow and thrash it out before I have to give an answer."

The two men agreed to follow this plan. Shortly after Mr. Webster had returned to his desk, he had a note from Mr. Peabody indicating that Mr. Eustis had indeed made an appointment to see the director of the library on the following afternoon.

How do you evaluate the positions taken by Mr. Eustis and Mr. Webster respectively with regard to reference assistance to students and retention of *Book Review Digest* and similar sources on the open shelves? What are the arguments on either side?

If you were Mr. Webster, what recommendation would you make to Mr. Peabody, and how would you support it?

12 An Admirer
of Grant

The X_____ State Library, located in the capital city of a large western state, serves in the dual capacity of a reference library for the legislative and executive branches of the government, and a library extension agency for residents of the state. The library has a large general book collection numbering more than 700,000 cataloged volumes. This collection is designed to supplement local library resources throughout the state, and is carefully selected to ensure that the more scholarly, specialized and expensive books of importance will be available through interlibrary loan to public libraries. In addition to providing less frequently used materials to the patrons of the state's public libraries from its own resources, the library also serves as a clearinghouse for interlibrary loan requests.

The X_____ State Library houses an extensive collection of United States public documents, including the complete Congressional edition. Until 1923, the library received all of the publications of the federal government which were available to depository libraries. Although it now serves only as a selective depository, the collection of government documents is very complete for the period up to 1940. Since none of the public or academic libraries in the state have any significant holdings of government publications, the State Library has made a special effort to build up its collection of documents, with particular emphasis on early government publications before 1900. These extensive resources have been carefully cataloged and organized, although for more recent publications there has been a tendency to employ briefer cataloging, and to depend on published indexes to locate individual documents. The library's reference collection includes all of the bibliographic resources and special indexes which are necessary to service and utilize these collections effectively.

Walter Tyler has served as head of the reference department at the X_____ State Library for nearly ten years. Although the library provides little in the way of direct reference service to the public, large numbers of inquiries are handled by mail each week. These include both inquiries from smaller libraries that have limited reference resources, and occasional letters from individuals who live in very small communities or in rural areas where public library service is either very poor or nonexistent.

One morning, Mr. Tyler found the following letter among a group of items sent to his desk by the State Librarian for reply. The letter was addressed to the State Librarian, and bore the postmark of a small, rural community in the northwest corner of the state.

Dear Sir:

For years now since my retirement from business I have been very interested in studying about the Civil War, and the career of the great leader of the Union Armies, General Grant. Just recently, I have been reading a book about his later years.

As you know, after his second term, Grant retired, and was forced to live for a number of years in real poverty. I am sorry to say that it was not until shortly before his death in 1885 that President Cleveland signed a bill which restored him to the rank of General of the Army, and provided a government pension as a token of the nation's gratitude. I understand that some of the General's friends in Congress had attempted several years previous to give him back his old rank and to obtain a pension for him, and that a bill was introduced to this effect in the Congress as early as 1880. I read somewhere that one of the Congressmen, whose name I think was Cook, made a fine speech in support of this bill which was defeated.

I am writing to you to find out if there is any way to locate a copy of that speech Mr. Cook made. I realize that this may be hard to find, since I am not certain of the date. I have talked to Miss Margaret Troy our Town Librarian about this and she tells me that you people have copies of all of the records of Congress in your library. Miss Troy said that if you could find this speech that she thought you could have a copy made for me. This is something that I would really like to have, and if you are not too busy I would appreciate your doing this for me.

Thank you. I expect that I will have to pay something for this, so kindly let me know about any charges in advance.

Yours truly,
Everett B. Livermore

The solution to this case consists of locating the document to which Mr. Livermore's letter refers, if indeed it exists. Your analysis should include an outline of the steps necessary to solve this problem, and an indication of the reference sources consulted to locate the item. Does the fact that this inquiry must be handled by mail present any problems?

13 Aid to
an Author

The C_____ Public Library is located in a large city in one of the eastern seaboard states. C_____ is primarily an industrial community, with a population of nearly 300,000, including many who reside in suburban towns and unincorporated areas outside of the city limits. The major industries include steel and other heavy metals, automobile assembly and shipbuilding. Although C_____ is an older city, and has a large and heterogeneous population, one finds little evidence of the urban blight in downtown areas that is so often characteristic of similar cities. This is due largely to a progressive and enlightened municipal administration which has used both local and federal funds to great advantage in renewal programs. This attitude has attracted new industry to the city, and has tended to create a climate where business can flourish.

The C_____ Public Library has also benefited from the progressive and farsighted municipal administration. It occupies a spacious new building, completed two years ago. The book collection of 350,000 volumes reflects careful attention on the part of the professional staff to weeding and replacement of outdated materials. The library has 31 professionals on its staff, most of whom are library school graduates. A supporting clerical staff of 44 makes it possible for members of the professional staff to devote the greater part of their time to the more creative aspects of organizing and servicing an active book collection. The library maintains six branches, and also provides extension service to the unincorporated areas adjacent to the city by means of bookmobiles and deposit stations.

The C_____ Public Library is organized for public service along subject divisional lines. The three major departments are Arts and

Literature, Social Sciences (including history), and Business and Technology.

The staff of the Social Sciences Division has responsibility both for selecting books and journals and for providing reference service in such subject fields as sociology, psychology, religion, archaeology, anthropology, government and history. The C_____ Public Library is a partial depository for United States government publications. Most of these are not cataloged, but are housed in pamphlet boxes or vertical files adjacent to the Social Sciences Reading Room. The reference collection is a good one. It includes all of the general indexes and bibliographic tools that one might expect to find in a large and well-supported public library.

Robert Jackson is the junior professional member of the staff of three librarians in the Social Sciences Department. He is 27 years old, and has spent two years in the Social Sciences Department at C_____. This is his first professional library experience.

One evening as Mr. Jackson was completing a period of duty at the public service desk, a tall, well-dressed and rather distinguished looking man entered the reading room. After browsing for a few minutes among some new books which were on display, the man approached the desk, and introduced himself.

"Hello, I don't think that I've seen you here before, although I use this library quite a good deal. My name is Ed Kirkwood. I live out in the suburbs, but my office is here in town."

"Happy to meet you. I'm Bob Jackson."

"Glad to know you, Mr. Jackson. You people certainly have a fine library here. I've never been up in this part of the building before. I do most of my reading downstairs in the Business Library. As a matter of fact, the young lady down there suggested that I come up here. She thought that you might have the more general books, and that's what I need."

"I see. What type of material are you looking for?"

"Well, I'm afraid that's fairly complicated. In fact, I probably ought to come back during the day when you have more time."

"We're not too busy right now, so why don't you let me try to help you tonight. If we can't find what you're looking for now, we can hunt it up first thing in the morning."

"That's awfully kind of you. I'm not even sure that it's possible to find the kind of thing I'm after. First of all, let me explain that for some time now I've made a hobby of studying law. One aspect of law I've been especially interested in is the problem of invasion of privacy. I've studied all the laws of wiretapping, and the question of whether or not evidence obtained by wiretapping should be admissible in court. I suppose you're familiar with this question?"

"Actually, I don't know too much about it, except for what I've been able to gather from some occasional editorials and magazine articles."

"Well, as you can imagine, from a legal point of view it's very complex. I've read all of the law and opinions on this that I've been able to get my hands on. In fact, I'm supposed to be kind of an expert on the subject."

"You certainly must have made quite a study of it."

"Yes, but only in relation to the law and the courts. Now, I have a friend who is on the staff of one of the big magazines. Not a legal magazine, but one of the better popular ones. He has suggested that I write an article about wiretapping, and he thinks his magazine might publish it. Now the problem is, I don't think that an article full of legal citations is going to make very interesting reading for the general public, do you?"

"Yes, I think you're right about that."

"What I'd like to do is to survey some of the different opinions about wiretapping, to try to evaluate the pros and cons, especially from the point of view of some of the more liberal groups. By the same token, I'd want to consider the conservative point of view as well. But, although I've read a good deal of this material casually in the past, now that I need it, I haven't the faintest idea of how to find it again. I suppose that most of it is in magazines and pamphlets. So, what I'd like to find out is, how should I begin?"

"I'm afraid that you'd have to wade through a good deal of material."

"Oh, I don't mind that. I've got time to read. It's just that I don't know how to go about finding it."

"That's where we might be able to help you. Let me see now, you would be interested chiefly in magazine and newspaper articles, and in pamphlets, particularly those that express strong opinions either for or against wiretapping?"

"That's right. I'd really like to consider as many of the arguments for and against as I can."

"I suppose there must be books on the subject. And, of course, you'd probably want to look at state and federal documents. I do know that a good many laws have been proposed about wiretapping, and I should think that we could find some material in Congressional hearings or the *Congressional Record*. That would cover current points of view fairly well. Would you be interested in the history of wiretapping too?"

"I ought to cover it at least briefly. I think probably one or two good, objective histories would do. Do you think I could find this easily?"

"You could find it, but it might not be too easy. You'd have to search through a number of indexes both to periodicals and to documents, and I'm afraid that some of them aren't too easy to use. I'll tell you what. Suppose we could put together a reading list for you, perhaps a dozen or so titles you could look at. We could choose things that would reflect several different points of view about the problem, and give you some of the background information as well."

"That would be wonderful. Of course, you wouldn't have to worry about including legal opinions or that sort of thing, because I'm quite familiar with those. But, I couldn't ask you to go to all that trouble for me."

"Actually, it wouldn't be too difficult for us. Suppose you give me your name and home telephone number, and let me take a few days to get this list together for you. I'll call you when I have it ready."

Mr. Kirkwood thanked Mr. Jackson more than once for his offer of help before he left the library. Jackson again promised to telephone him as soon as the list had been prepared.

Next day, Mr. Jackson discussed his conversation of the previous evening with Mrs. Logan, the head of the Social Sciences Department. He said that he wondered if he had perhaps been a bit rash in offering to prepare a reading list for Mr. Kirkwood, since he realized that compiling such a list might require a good deal of time.

If you were the department head in this case, how would you respond to Mr. Jackson's final question? Is it customary for a public library to offer to provide such a service for its patrons? Do you feel that the kind and amount of service that a public library should provide depends on the identity of the inquirer, or should there be general policies establishing limits? In the absence of such a policy statement in this case, did Mr. Jackson have the right to offer to draw up a reading list without consulting first with his supervisor?

How would you comment on Mr. Jackson's handling of the reference interview in this case?

Assuming that the reading list is to be compiled, what sources would it be appropriate for Mr. Jackson to use, and in what order should they be consulted? How much time would be required to draw up an adequate reading list?

14 Reorganizing a Collection of Documents

The University of X_____ is located in a large city in the western United States. As a publicly supported institution, the university has responded as fully as possible to post-World War II pressures for expansion, and thus, has experienced a boom during the past twenty years, which has manifested itself in an apparently endless cycle of doubled, trebled and quadrupled enrollments, and frantic construction of new buildings in an effort to provide facilities for a veritable horde of students. Enrollment has grown from 900 undergraduates in 1946 to a current level of 4,500 undergraduate day students, nearly 900 graduate students, and some 5,000 or more students enrolled in evening and extension courses. At last year's commencement, the university awarded 1,143 baccalaureate degrees in the liberal arts and sciences, engineering, business administration and education; 67 master's degrees in the liberal arts, 206 in education, 41 in business administration, 31 in engineering; and 11 doctorates in engineering and science. At present, graduate programs are offered at the master's level in education, English literature, history, sociology, economics, government, music, chemistry, physics, geology, engineering (civil, mechanical, electrical and nuclear), and business administration, and doctoral programs in engineering, chemistry, and physics. A doctoral program in education is also planned for the immediate future.

The X_____ University Library has been caught up in a cycle of increasing demands for library services from a growing student population, and in particular has had to face great pressures in response to the rapid inauguration of graduate programs, which have required vast strengthening of library resources. The book and periodical collection has grown in 15 years from 88,000 to 275,000 cataloged volumes. The rate of current acquisition is approximately 19,000 volumes annually, and, even at this, the library is still unable to keep up with the demand for materials on the part of students and faculty.

Fortunately, while the library has had to face many serious problems, it has also enjoyed the full and enthusiastic support of the president and trustees of the university, and has received each year a generous portion of the university budget. The most tangible expression of this support came two years ago, with the completion of a new $4,000,000 library building, centrally located on a compact instructional campus. The new building has been artfully planned to achieve maximum economies in terms of staff, while providing nearly complete flexibility in the arrangement of space and services to meet future needs. The capacity of the building, as it stands, is 500,000 volumes, although space for an additional 250,000 volumes is available, when needed, on the upper floors, which are presently used for classrooms. The building has attracted national attention in both the library and the educational press as a model of contemporary design.

The library staff is organized along functional lines, in terms of the usual public and technical services activities, and numbers 57 full-time employees, of whom 23 are professional librarians. In addition to the director and assistant director of the library, the professional staff is divided as follows:

Technical Services

1 chief of technical services
5 catalogers
2 serials librarians
3 acquisitions librarians

Public Services

1 chief of public services
2 circulation librarians
3 reference librarians
1 inter-library loan librarian
1 audio-visual librarian
1 reserve book librarian
1 departmental librarian for the education library, which is not housed in the central building.

The director of the library, Dr. Gardner, is both a distinguished scholar and a competent administrator. He enjoys excellent relations with the administration of the university, the faculty, students and alumni. Dr. Gardner prefers to devote himself to the larger questions of library policy, budget, funding and the like, and has delegated day-by-day responsibility for internal administration to Mr. Oakland, the assistant director. Mr. Oakland is a youngish man, who came to his present position after seven years of professional experience in a variety of technical services posts on the staff of a large university library. Oakland is generally considered an able and talented man. He is both liked and respected by the library staff and indeed throughout the university community.

Mr. Oakland has full responsibility, under the general guidance of Dr. Gardner, for every area of library operations. The chief of technical services, Mr. Linton, and the chief of public services, Miss Morgan, are directly responsible to him. They, in turn, administer their respective areas of service, and have considerable independent authority to make decisions in terms of general policies established by Mr. Oakland and Dr. Gardner. Both Mr. Linton and Miss Morgan are comparatively young people, and, like Mr. Oakland, neither has had extensive library experience. Mr. Linton spent several years after graduation from college working as a salesman, received his library science degree when he was 31 years old, and subsequently served for two years as administrative assistant to the head of the catalog department at a large eastern university library before coming to X_____ a year ago. He faced the immediate problem of effecting a complete reorganization of the library's technical services arm which was, according to Mr. Oakland, "still trying to operate with horse and buggy methods." In the short span of one year, Mr. Linton has succeeded in lifting the technical services division out of the doldrums, and has made great strides in the development of an efficient operation. He has made extensive use of machine techniques in the area of book purchasing, so that acquisitions have been placed on a current basis for the first time in 20 years, while at the same time the library has achieved a far greater measure of control over its book funds and accounting procedures. By virtue of persistent effort, he and his staff have steadily whittled away at an arrearage of nearly 20,000 volumes that had existed in the catalog department and that, prior to his coming, had seemed destined to grow to the point of choking off the entire operation. All of this has been accomplished without any significant additions to the full-time staff, through the introduction of machine techniques, whenever possible, and by subjecting operations in the technical services department to the most rigorous scrutiny, so as to make certain that every moment of the working day was being used to maximum advantage by the members of the professional staff, and every task that could possibly be reassigned to a clerk or a student assistant was taken out of the hands of the professional staff. While Mr. Linton encountered some resistance among the staff at first, particularly with a few individuals who had been in the library for many years and who resented his somewhat cavalier approach to established routines, these attitudes changed rapidly as the results of his efforts became apparent. Morale, which had been at a low ebb in the department, improved almost at once, and Mr. Linton became a kind of popular hero with his own staff, as well as the object of a good deal of favorable comment throughout the library.

Miss Morgan has done an equally satisfactory job as chief of public services, although her success has been less spectacular than Mr. Linton's. She is 30 years old, and has had six years of professional experience, including two years as a reference assistant in a large public library, and four years as librarian in a research laboratory attached to one of the nation's leading philanthropic foundations. She came to X_____ from the latter post six months ago, and has made a favorable impression both on the library administration and on the staff in her initial experience in an academic library.

One morning, Miss Morgan received in her office mail a memorandum from the assistant director which read as follows:

TO: Miss Morgan
FROM: Simon Oakland
RE: Proposed reorganization of government documents collections

Attached is a copy of a proposed statement of policy for the handling of government documents in this library which has been prepared by Mr. Linton, after a careful investigation of this problem, undertaken some weeks ago at my request. I am sure you must be aware of the fact that the processing of documents has, for some years, left much to be desired, while at the same time representing an enormous, and ever-growing burden in the technical services division. Indeed, this problem has become so serious that I have asked Mr. Linton to re-examine all of our present procedures with respect to documents, and to recommend major changes wherever he concludes that these might be appropriate.

The results of his investigations, and his recommendations, are incorporated in the attached report. Some of his proposals are, to be sure, quite radical, yet I find myself drawn to them very strongly, and I am, at the moment, giving serious consideration to accepting and implementing them. I realize, however, that the public service areas of the library, and particularly the reference service, would be affected, and, therefore, I should value your reactions to these proposals from the reference point of view. You will note that Mr. Linton has limited himself to a consideration of the problem solely in terms of his own area of responsibility, the technical services. From this standpoint, the economies that might be realized from the implementation of his proposals are impressive, yet I would not wish to accept these recommendations if you feel that they would adversely affect service to faculty and students.

I would appreciate it if you would examine this report carefully, discuss it with members of your staff, and bring me your reactions to it, from a reference point of view, in the form of a memorandum no later than one week from today, since I am facing a deadline in the preparation of next year's budget, which will require substantial modification if Mr. Linton's recommendations are accepted.

Attached to the memorandum from Mr. Oakland was a copy of a long typewritten report prepared by Mr. Linton titled "Proposals for the Reorganization of the Documents Collection in the University of X_____ Library." The report began with an examination of the scope of the existing collection of documents. Mr. Linton estimated that, at present, the library housed approximately 30,000 documents, and that perhaps 95 percent of these were federal government documents, the remainder being state and United Nations documents. He pointed out that during the preceding academic year, the library had received nearly 9,000 individual items in the category of documents, most of which emanated from the federal government.

Federal documents were obtained by the University of X_____ Library in several ways, the most important of which was the depository privilege. As a partial depository library, the university received regular shipments from the Government Printing Office of publications in certain pre-selected series. Many additional titles were acquired by other means. Some of these were non-depository items, sent to the library by individual government agencies, and frequently unsolicited. Also included in this category were subscriptions to government periodicals, a few individual documents ordered at the request of members of the faculty, older documents obtained through commercial agencies, occasionally in microform, in response to specific faculty or staff requests, and titles sent to the library by members of Congress.

Mr. Linton pointed out that the number of documents acquired annually was growing with each passing year, and that the library had been feeling increased pressures from the faculty, as a result of curriculum development, to expand its holdings on both a current and a retrospective basis. All indications were that the library might well anticipate, within the next ten years, that annual acquisitions of documents would increase to a figure of perhaps 15,000 or more items.

The report next turned to a consideration of the handling of documents after these were received by the library. All shipments of documents were handled initially by a senior clerical assistant in the acquisitions department who sorted them into the following categories:

1. Periodicals. These were turned over to the serials librarians who entered them in the visible periodicals index, and shelved them in the appropriate area of the stacks. The serials librarians also had responsibility for seeing to it that government periodicals, along with all other periodicals, were assembled for binding at the appropriate time, and that bound volumes were entered in the public catalog and the shelf list.

2. Titles in series which were regularly cataloged. The acquisitions clerk was sufficiently experienced to be able to recognize these most of the time. As individual items in this category arrived, they were turned over to the catalogers for descriptive cataloging and the assignment of decimal classification numbers. They were represented in the public catalog by individual entries, as well as by series cards. Some series were kept together on the shelves, and bore the same classification number, as, for example, the *Bulletin* series of the Women's Bureau of the Department of Labor. Other titles were classified individually, according to subject, as, for example, the annual issues of the *Yearbook of Agriculture*.

3. Individual documents ordered by members of the faculty or library staff. These were identified by having a clerical assistant check outstanding order files with the remaining documents in hand, after items in categories 1 and 2 above had been separated out. All items in this category were automatically cataloged and classified, bound or placed in protective covers, and shelved either in the general book collection or on the reserve book shelves for a specific course, according to the direction given by the person who had originally requested the document. Items in microform were shelved, after cataloging, in the microfilm room.

4. All remaining documents, after those in the above categories had been eliminated, were routed to the acquisitions librarians, who, periodically, examined them. Items which appeared to be of some substance were sent to the catalog department for descriptive cataloging and classification, subsequently bound or placed in protective covers, and ultimately incorporated into the collection. Pamphlets of doubtful value, or on subjects not related to the instructional program, were routed to the reference librarian, and it is presumed that most of these eventually found their way into the information files.

Mr. Linton noted in his report that exclusive of periodicals, a total of 3,213 documents had received full cataloging during the preceding year. He pointed out that this figure represented approximately 20 percent of the total annual work load of the catalog department, and that nearly one-third of the items in the 10,000-title backlog of work which currently rested on the shelves of the catalog department were government documents.

Mr. Linton proposed that, as a solution to this problem, the X_____ University Library abandon forthwith the cataloging and classification of newly acquired government documents, and that, henceforth, no additional documents be represented in the public catalogs, or the shelf list. He further proposed that a documents division be established, to be housed in a space in the building not currently being used for other purposes, and adequate to provide for a small public reading room, a work room, and adjacent book stack shelving for approximately 20,000 volumes. The proposed documents division would have responsibility for the following major activities:

1. The acquisition of all documents—international, federal, state, and local—requested by members of the faculty and staff.

2. The initial sorting of all documents received by the library, either through the depository privilege, by virtue of purchase orders, or by gift.

3. The organization of *all* federal government documents received by the library, regardless of the manner in which obtained, into a single collection arranged on the shelves in accordance with the Documents Office Classification System. He proposed that as each federal document was received, the assistant in the documents division locate the appropriate entry for the item in the *Monthly Catalog*, make a check mark in the *Monthly Catalog* to indicate that the document had been received, and mark the document in a conspicuous place with the Documents Office classification number. All federal documents would be treated in this manner routinely, and no conventional cataloging or classification of documents would occur. The annotated master copy of the *Monthly Catalog* would serve as the library's public and official record of its holdings of federal documents. The monthly and annual indexes to the *Monthly Catalog* would provide access to individual documents in the collection from a subject point of view, and would take the place of individual subject entries which had previously been made in the public catalogs.

4. Evaluate all non-federal documents received by the library, route important documents to the catalog department for conventional cataloging and classification, and send the remainder to the reference staff either for inclusion in the information files or for discard as they saw fit. Mr. Linton pointed out that the number of non-federal documents received by the library was small enough so that these might be

handled in the conventional manner without serious burden on the technical services department.

5. Maintain necessary check-in records for individual issues of U.S. Government periodicals, which were also to be handled in the same manner as federal documents.

6. Be responsible for identifying both serial publications and monographic materials in the documents collection that required binding, and forward these to the chief of technical services for inclusion in the library's general binding order.

7. Provide reference assistance to individual members of the university faculty, staff, and student body in locating documents and using them in the documents division reading room. This would include maintenance of any federal documents acquired in microform, and Mr. Linton proposed that reading machines be transferred from the microfilm room to the new documents division for this purpose.

8. Arrange for photocopies to be made of any federal documents required for reserve shelves, and forward these to the circulation librarians. As part of the library's reference service, the documents division would also have responsibility for arranging for the photocopying of federal documents for individuals requesting this service.

Mr. Linton noted in his report that the proposed documents division might be questioned in terms of the library's existing administrative structure, as to whether or not responsibility for it should lie with the chief of technical services or with the chief of public services, since the division would have functions in both areas. He indicated that he had no specific recommendation to make in this matter, since he felt that the decision should be made at a higher administrative level, but that he personally saw no reason why the documents division might not be incorporated into the public services arm of the library if this was the wish of the director. He suggested that a professional librarian be added to the staff on a full-time basis to take responsibility for the division, and that appropriate clerical and student assistance be provided to handle the routines as outlined and to assist readers during the hours of library service. Mr. Linton indicated that he saw no reason why the public service desk in the proposed documents division could not be staffed by student assistants during the evening and on weekends, in accordance with the prevailing library practice of staffing all public service desks, including the general reference desk, in this manner at these times.

Mr. Linton proposed that these new procedures for handling government documents be instituted at the earliest possible date, with the transfer of approximately 3,000 documents now awaiting conventional cataloging in the technical services division to the documents division, to form the nucleus of the new collection to be arranged by Documents Office classification number as outlined above. All documents received by the library in the future would also be routed to the documents division for handling in the same manner.

The report next turned to the subject of the estimated 30,000 or more federal documents presently in the collection of the library. He noted that these documents were currently scattered in a variety of places and pointed out that one of the great merits of his proposal was that, in the future, all newly acquired federal documents would be in one place, and thus, the problem of locating them would be greatly simplified for users of the library. As for the documents presently in the collection, these fell in the following categories:

1. Government periodicals, presently shelved with the general periodicals collection. Mr. Linton estimated that no more than 200 of the approximately 1,400 periodicals currently received by the library fell into this category. He recommended that government periodicals be removed from the general collection, and transferred en bloc to the new documents division.

2. Cataloged and classified documents presently incorporated in the general book collection of the library, of which, Mr. Linton estimated there might be 25,000 or more individual titles. He indicated that, ideally, he would like to recommend that each of these documents be identified, all catalog cards removed from the public catalogs and the shelf list, and the documents themselves transferred to the documents division, checked off in the annotated copies of the *Monthly Catalog*, and shelved by Documents Office classification number in the new documents collection. Unfortunately, such a task would be far beyond the capacity of his staff at the present time, or, indeed, in the foreseeable future, so that he was compelled to suggest that this portion of the documents collection remain unchanged, and that the new procedures be applied only to documents presently awaiting cataloging or those received in the future. Linton noted that an analogous problem had arisen in other libraries by virtue of the changeover from one classification system to another, and that it was common practice to leave the existing book collection in the old classification system, while employing the new one for newly acquired materials, on the theory that older materials were not used often enough to merit the enormous costs involved in recataloging them. He said that this principle was especially applicable to federal government documents. Indeed, if it were necessary to recatalog the existing documents collection in this manner, the entire value of his plan, in terms of its economies, would be lost, and it would be better to continue present procedures.

3. Cataloged and classified documents in the reference collection of

the library. Mr. Linton proposed that these be transferred to the documents division, and that, in the interests of consistency, all federal government publications acquired in the future for reference purposes be incorporated in the new documents collection.

4. Cataloged and classified documents presently on reserve book shelves for assigned readings in specific courses. Mr. Linton proposed that the originals of these gradually be shifted to the new documents collection, and that photocopies be substituted on the reserve book shelves, the photocopies to be discarded when no longer needed for reserve purposes.

5. Uncataloged documents arranged by subject in file folders in the information files, administered and maintained by the reference department. Mr. Linton proposed that no effort be made to reorganize the documents in this category, since these were presumably of only marginal value to the instructional program of the college, else they would have been cataloged and classified in the first place. Under his plan, of course, no more federal documents would be added to the information files, and those currently in the files would presumably be weeded out in time and discarded.

The report concluded with the following summary of the proposals:

In summary, I should like to review briefly the proposal that I have made above for the organization of government documents in the light of the benefits to be derived from it. First, all federal documents would be housed in a single area of the library, arranged in a simple classified order so as to be readily available to faculty and students. In contrast to this, the present arrangement of documents, scattered as they are by subject or by form throughout the general book collection, means that an individual seeking a specific item must look in five or six different places in order to determine whether or not the library owns the document. I submit that most people are not aware, nor can they be expected to be aware, that there are a half dozen places in the library where a given document might be found. Under the scheme I have proposed, the individual seeking a federal document would know that there is only one place in the library where it could be, in the documents division. (I realize that there would, unfortunately, be some unavoidable exceptions to this under my plan, but feel nonetheless, that location and use of documents by the public would be greatly simplified).

Secondly, from the point of view of students and faculty, the plan would offer enormous advantages in terms of the promptness with which newly acquired documents would be made available on the shelves. At present, because of the backlog of work in the catalog department, and also because of the difficulties involved in the descriptive cataloging of government documents, I estimate that an average of four to six months elapses between the time a document arrives in the library and the time

it reaches the shelves. There are, right now, some 3,000 documents awaiting processing. Many of these have been on the shelves for more than a
year, and some, I regret to say, have been awaiting cataloging for two or
three years. In many of these cases, the document contains statistical
material which is valuable only because it is current, so that a delay of
many months in getting the item on the shelves is crucial. Because of
the difficulties involved in the conventional cataloging of government
documents, such as the problem of corporate authorship, the necessity of
maintaining series cards in the public catalog, and the like, clerical and
student assistants are able to make little or no contribution to the processing
of these materials, so that a staggering amount of professional staff time is
devoted to getting an individual document on the shelves. I cannot help
but feel that often the amount of time required to catalog a given document is completely out of proportion to the intrinsic value of the document
itself. Under the plan I have proposed, I see no reason why an individual
document would not be available on the shelves for public use on the day
it arrived in the library, since no cataloging or classification would be involved, or, at the very least, on the day following its arrival. This is in
contrast to the present waiting period of several months, or, in some cases,
even years.

I should also make note of the great advantages that would be derived
from having all responsibility for documents centered in a single office. All
questions relating to documents might then be referred to a single person
who would be in a position to be quite knowledgeable about every aspect
of our operations, since acquisition, organization and use of documents
would occur in a single place. Moreover, to catalog and classify documents,
rather than to accept and use a perfectly adequate classification system
and subject index already provided for us through the *Monthly Catalog,*
strikes me as a luxury this library can no longer afford. As you know, we
have an enormous backlog of work in the technical services division, and in
spite of our best efforts during the past year, thousands of titles are still
awaiting cataloging. I feel that we have exhausted every available technique for speeding up operations and that some major and fundamental
changes are necessary if we are ever to have the hope of getting out from
under, and putting our operations on a current basis. As I look to the
future, I see only the prospect of larger and larger numbers of books being
acquired each year, and I do not feel that I can, in all conscience, recommend the substantial increases in the staff of the technical services division
that would be necessary to handle our anticipated workload under existing
procedures. The adoption of these proposals with respect to government
documents would, I believe, mark a major breakthrough, and eliminate a
millstone that presently hangs about the neck of every member of the
catalog department, in addition to making for vastly improved service to
the public.

Miss Morgan read the report through twice in its entirety, and found
that her initial reactions to the proposal were mixed. From the point of

view of the technical services operation of the library, as she was aware of the problems Mr. Linton had to face, she realized that some sweeping changes would be necessary, if the work of the division were ever to be put on a current basis. She felt that the space in the building available to house the proposed documents division was adequate and satisfactory from a public service point of view. She agreed that substantial economies might be achieved through the implementation of Mr. Linton's proposals, which had the effect of making the cataloging and classification of government documents almost wholly a clerical operation, thus releasing the time of the professional staff in the technical services division for other duties. She realized that the alternative to this would be either to add substantially to the staff of the technical services division, or else abandon all hope of ever catching up with the backlog of work in cataloging and classification. From all of these points of view, Mr. Linton's proposal seemed to offer a logical solution to a complex problem. Moreover, it was certainly true that the delays in getting new government documents onto the shelves and available for use were a source of frequent complaint, especially among members of the faculty. Again, the prospect of having newly acquired documents on the shelves and ready for use a day or two after their arrival in the library was indeed attractive.

On the other hand, Miss Morgan felt some uncertainties about the plan. She was vaguely troubled at the prospect of separating federal documents from the general collection, and unsure about the elimination of documents from the card catalog. She wondered how frequently documents might be overlooked as potential source materials, especially by students, under the new plan, since they would not be listed in the catalog. She resolved to review Mr. Linton's proposals carefully during the next few days, before preparing the memorandum that Mr. Oakland had requested.

How should Miss Morgan respond to the proposal that Mr. Linton has made for the reorganization of the documents collection at the University of X_____ Library? What do you feel are the limitations, if any, of this proposal from a reference standpoint? Might it be modified in any way to make it more satisfactory from the point of view of the library's public service responsibilities, while at the same time preserving those features of the plan that are designed to resolve the problems of the catalog department? If you were Miss Morgan, what aspects of the problem would you feel it most important to bring to Mr. Oakland's attention, in order that he might make the soundest possible decision concerning Mr. Linton's proposal?

15 Meeting an Agency Deadline

L_____ and C_____ Associates is a medium sized advertising agency located in a large midwestern city. Returning from lunch one afternoon, Ethel Willits, librarian of the agency, found Roger Elgin, a young account executive, waiting in her office. Their conversation was as follows:

MISS WILLITS: "Hello, Roger. This is a pleasant surprise. Can I do something to help you?"

MR. ELGIN: "Ethel, I sure hope you can. I'm really in a jam. I need some material in a hurry."

MISS WILLITS: "Well, I'll be glad to try. What are you looking for?"

MR. ELGIN: "This probably will sound very strange, but would you have anything in the library on the history of waxed paper?"

MISS WILLITS: "I'll admit that is a little unusual, although after having been with this agency for eight years, nothing that you people ask for could surprise me. Can you give me some idea of what kind of material you need, or how you plan to use it?"

MR. ELGIN: "Sure! You probably know that the agency has been trying to get the Y_____ Manufacturing Company account for some time. They're one of these old New England firms, very conservative and traditional in their approach to business. Their idea of advertising, at least up until now, has been to mail a calendar with a picture of a covered bridge on it to each customer once a year."

MISS WILLITS: "I think you're exaggerating just a little bit."

MR. ELGIN: "Ethel, I'm not! Not one bit! They operate as though they were still in the nineteenth century. But, this is going to change, because they've just brought in a couple of younger men to head up their sales department. They're in the market for an agency and we'd like to be it. The problem is, not only are they conservative, but their products are pretty prosaic—like gears. It's pretty difficult to dream up a campaign that will glamourize the gear. I haven't been involved in this directly up until now, but we were discussing the problem of finding a theme for a campaign at the sales conference last Friday. And, instead of being sensible, and letting Kenilworth, who gets paid to worry about these things, solve the problem, I had to open my big mouth and make a suggestion."

MISS WILLITS: "And Mr. Kenilworth liked your suggestion and told you to go and work up a presentation?"

MR. ELGIN: "I wish he had. But, you know Kenilworth. He's the original Great Stone Face. He just nodded when I'd finished, and went on to the next item on the agenda. Then, just before lunch today, he called me in and told me that he'd been able to set up a meeting for five o'clock this afternoon with the people from Y_____ out at the airport. They're giving us an hour between planes. Apparently, they're on the way home from a trip out to the west coast. Kenilworth feels that this is our big opportunity, and wants me to make the basic presentation and show them at least one sample."

MISS WILLITS: "I gather that you don't have a sample presentation worked up."

MR. ELGIN: "Right. That's my problem. He never gave the slightest indication last Friday that he wanted me to prepare a presentation."

MISS WILLITS: "What does all this have to do with waxed paper?"

MR. ELGIN: "The theme I suggested was *practicality*. My idea was to build a series of ads around great *practical* inventions of the past."

MISS WILLITS: "Like waxed paper?"

MR. ELGIN: "Yes, waxed paper, the thermos bottle, things like that. A little biography of the inventor and the story of how he came to invent waxed paper. Illustrated with some nineteenth century prints showing people using waxed paper. And, showing how the products of the Y_____ Company are the twentieth century equivalent, in terms of *their* practicality."

MISS WILLITS: "Let me see if I've got this straight now. You want a biography of the inventor of waxed paper, and the story of how he came to invent it. For a meeting late this afternoon."

MR. ELGIN: "And some pictures of people using it. Pictures are important. Period stuff, not people in modern dress. Or, I could probably use the thermos bottle instead of waxed paper, if you think that would be easier to find. Can you possibly get this together within an hour or two? I'm free this afternoon, and I could help you research it, if you'll just tell me how to go about it."

L____ and C____ Associates serves the advertising needs of about twenty major clients, as well as several score smaller accounts. Its library has existed for fifteen years, and is staffed by a librarian, Miss Willits, and a secretary. The library subscribes to approximately 300 magazines and newspapers, about half of which are retained permanently in bound form. The remaining periodicals and newspapers are scanned and clipped for a "data file" which fills twenty-five large file cabinets. The library has about 2,000 books, including almanacs, yearbooks and other sources of current information and statistics. Subjects most heavily represented in the book collection include nutrition and food, health, insurance, beverages and marketing, reflecting the interests of the firm's principal clients. Recent books and trade journals in advertising are, of course, included in substantial numbers. The city of 150,000 people in which the agency is located has an excellent public library.

Can you locate the information that Mr. Elgin is seeking in this case? Where can the kind of biographical, historical and illustrative materials that he needs be found? Can a satisfactory collection of material be assembled within the time available for solution of the problem? In what ways might Mr. Elgin participate in the search? What kinds of special files and indexes, beyond those described in the case, would you expect to find in a library of this kind that would aid in solving the problem?

16 A Proverbial

Phrase

"Miss Proctor, could I bother you for a minute?" Alice Proctor, assistant reference librarian of the University of Z_____ Library, looked up from the book reviewing journal she had been scanning to find a young woman, apparently a student, standing in front of the reference desk. "Of course. How can I help you?"

"Well, you probably don't remember me, but I'm in Dr. Clayton's research methods class. You spoke to our class a few weeks ago."

"Oh, yes. You're a graduate student, then. In history?"

"That's right, American colonial history, actually. I know that you must be very busy, and I wouldn't be bothering you now, except that I'm frankly just stumped, and I thought you might be able to advise me."

"I'm afraid that I'm not much of an historian, but I'll be glad to try."

"Do you know if there are any books in the library on sayings?"

"Sayings?"

"Yes. Like, old sayings, you know. 'A stitch in time saves nine,' that sort of thing."

"Oh, I see. You mean proverbs."

"Proverbs, that's right. How would I go about finding out what a proverb means?"

"Well, I think I'd try a dictionary. Is it an English proverb?"

"I don't know. Actually, I think it might be Irish."

"Why don't you try a dictionary?"

"I already have. I've looked in all of them."

"You've looked in all of the dictionaries in the reference collection?"

"Yes, I have."

At that moment, the telephone on Miss Proctor's desk rang.

"I'm afraid you'll have to excuse me for a moment. Why don't you take a look in the *Dictionary of English Proverbs?* You'll find it over there, next to the other English language dictionaries. If you don't find what you're looking for, come back and I'll try to help you."

Miss Proctor answered her telephone call, which was from a member of the faculty who had a particularly complex reference question that required no less than three trips to the card catalog before it was satisfactorily resolved. The next few minutes were busy ones for Miss Proctor, because, while she had been working on the telephone question, several students who needed reference help had been waiting. Since the reference room at the University of Z_____ Library was a large one, and the reference books were arranged on wall shelves all around the room, a good deal of walking was required, and nearly half an hour elapsed before Miss Proctor was free to return to her desk. At that point, she was again confronted by the young graduate student who had been seeking information about proverbs. "Well, did you have any luck with the proverbs?"

"No, I couldn't find a thing. I think I'll give up. It's hopeless. I've looked everywhere."

"Let's see, you said you thought this might be an Irish proverb?"

"It might be."

"I don't know if we have anything on Irish proverbs, or not. Let me look in the card catalog."

Miss Proctor left her desk, walked to the card catalog, and searched for entries under the subject heading "Proverbs, Irish." She found no cards bearing this heading, so she returned to the reference desk where the student was waiting for her, "We don't seem to have a thing on Irish proverbs. What is the proverb, anyway?"

"Well, actually, it's just a phrase—'the Irish Treasurer's Waggons,' and 'Waggons' is spelled with two g's."

"Is that all there is to the proverb? Just, 'the Irish Treasurer's Waggons,' nothing else?"

"That's all there is. It must have been some kind of a saying, don't you think?"

"It might be. Where did you find this saying? Is it in print somewhere?"

"I suppose it must be. To tell you the truth, I didn't find it, myself. But, one of the people in my seminar came across it, and we got to talking about it after the last class. We all wondered what could be inside the wagons that would be so frightening."

"Frightening?"

"Yes. As I remember it—oh, wait a minute, I wrote it down—here it is: 'These alarums reached even to the House of Burgesses, whose representatives are as affrighted as tho exposed to the Contents of the Irish Treasurer's Waggons.' I think that's the way it was read to the class. None of us had ever heard that expression before, and Professor Kent said he couldn't ever remember having come across it, either. So, I thought there might be some place where it would explain what was in the wagons, what the phrase means."

"This is Professor Kent's seminar in colonial history?"

"That's right."

Assuming that the reference collection at University of Z——— Library contains the standard sources that one might expect to find in any respectable large university library, how would you go about locating an explanation of the phrase in which the student is interested? Describe in detail all of the steps necessary to find a satisfactory solution to the problem.

Bearing in mind that this is a busy reference desk, and that Miss Proctor is alone, would you, under these circumstances, limit the search in any way? How would you comment on Miss Proctor's handling of the reference interview thus far?

17 Telephone
Reference Service

The A_____ Public Library serves an industrial and residential community of 65,000, located along the eastern seaboard of the United States. A_____ is not a particularly wealthy community, and during recent years it has been in something of a decline, losing population and tax revenue to the more attractive suburban cities and towns, as well as large unincorporated "county" areas that surround it. This population shift has occasioned a variety of governmental problems, not the least of which has been increased competition among municipal agencies for a diminishing supply of tax dollars.

In this atmosphere of municipal economy, the A_____ Public Library, under the direction of its librarian, Bertha Warren, has fared amazingly well. During the past ten years, the library budget has increased from $90,000 to nearly $200,000 and two new branch libraries have been constructed. Library facilities include three branches, a bookmobile, and a spacious, attractive central building with an excellent location in the heart of the city's business district. The financial success of the library is attributable in large measure to Miss Warren's distinguished administrative leadership, which has emphasized careful attention to public relations with a special effort to cultivate the support of city officials and community organizations. In this process, Miss Warren has had the benefit of the unqualified support of both her board of trustees and an active and enthusiastic friends of the library organization.

The professional staff of the A_____ Public Library numbers ten, in addition to Miss Warren. These include an assistant librarian, Miss Darby, who is also in charge of technical services, a cataloger, a bookmobile librarian, two branch librarians (the third branch, which is very small, is administered by a clerk), two childrens librarians, Miss

Temple and Miss Alton, a chief of reference service, Mrs. Madison, her assistant, Mr. Sherman, and an adult services librarian, Miss Lufkin. Not all of these people have had library school training. Several are senior members of the staff who entered the service of the library at a time when formal training was less common than it is today. In general, the staff is competent, the individuals on it are alert and interested in their jobs, and morale is excellent.

Every three weeks, the entire professional staff of the library participates in what has come to be known over the years as the "book meeting." The purpose of this meeting is to arrive at group decisions as to which books are to be purchased by the library, and in particular which new titles are to be bought in quantity in anticipation of heavy demand. Individual staff members are assigned general subject areas for which they are responsible in terms of reading and preparing brief reviews of newly published and forthcoming books. The meetings themselves are usually relaxed and pleasant occasions, marked by a good deal of lively conversation and interchange of opinion. From time to time, Miss Warren has used the book meeting both to inform members of the staff of trustee and administrative decisions that would affect them, and to allow an opportunity for discussion of problems of general interest outside of the area of book selection.

At one of these meetings, held in early April, Miss Warren, who was presiding, observed that the group had completed the immediate business at hand with respect to book purchases, and noting that some time remained before the customary closing hour, asked if there were other matters that those present would like to discuss.

MR. SHERMAN (Reference assistant): "Miss Warren, I have a problem that I would like very much to present this morning, both to you and to the other members of the group, if I may. Let me begin by saying that this is a problem I have already discussed thoroughly with Mrs. Madison, since she is my supervisor, and her feeling was that this would be an appropriate place to present it. Since it involves me most directly, I should like to begin the discussion, although I know that Mrs. Madison has had this same experience in the past many times, and she may want to add something to my presentation. I'm not sure that all of you here appreciate just how heavy the demands on the staff are after six o'clock on weekday evenings. To begin with, our smallest branch is not open in the evenings at all, and the other two branches are open only one evening a week. This means that after six, the central library is, in effect, providing the only library service available in the entire city.

"At central there is, as you know, Miss Warren, only one librarian on duty in the evenings, and that person is stationed in the reference room.

It is true that there are several clerks and student aides on duty too, but from the standpoint of professional service, the entire burden rests on the shoulders of the single reference person. Let me add that the children's room is, of course, closed after six p.m., too.

"Between six and nine on weekday evenings, it may surprise some of you to know that we have often had more than 300 people in this building. Use is particularly heavy the first four evenings of the week, and during school vacations. Last week, which happened to be spring vacation for most of the college students in the area, you couldn't get a seat either in the reference room or in the main reading room. Last Tuesday evening, which was my night on duty, I counted 111 reference questions, directional questions, and requests for assistance that came to me at the reference desk in less than three hours. As you can imagine, I was on the go all evening, and by the time nine o'clock rolled around, I was so tired I could hardly see straight. My point is that it was a pretty heavy evening's work for one person to handle.

"Almost half of those 111 reference questions that I mentioned a minute ago came in over the telephone, and this, of course, just made for an impossible situation. I simply could not get anything done. It just seemed as though every time I was in the middle of working with a patron at the reference desk, trying to learn how I could help him find the information he wanted, the foolish phone would ring. Now the thing about a ringing telephone is that you can't ignore it, so as a result the person who telephones is taken care of first, and the person who has taken the trouble to come down to the library is made to stand and wait. At one point, I had five people lined up in front of my desk, while I was tied up on the telephone for almost 15 minutes.

"Now, the thing that really annoyed me in all of this is that of those 60 or so phone calls that came to the reference desk on Tuesday evening, at least 30 were from *children*. This meant that on more than one occasion, an adult who had come to the library seeking reference assistance with a legitimate problem was kept waiting, while I was involved on the phone with some junior high school kid babbling about an English assignment. Well, just before eight o'clock, I finally realized that something had to give, so I went over to the main desk and told the people who handle the telephone not to put through any more calls to the reference room that evening, unless the calls were from adults. I told them to tell any child who called that he or she would have to come down to the library *in person* if they needed help, that we weren't going to try to handle any more of these questions over the phone. Well, it worked. So, the next evening that I was on duty, which was last Thursday, I tried it again—no telephone reference service unless the caller sounded like an adult. The result of this was that for the first time since school began last fall, I was able to give something like decent reference service. Instead of having to sandwich in reference work between telephone calls, I was able to devote myself primarily to the people, adults and teen-agers, who were actually *in the library*. Instead of having to try to answer a complicated reference question in 30 seconds, I could spend five or ten minutes with each person, and actually give them some assistance. Thursday was the first evening in a good many months when I really felt that I was doing the kind of reference work that I, and the library, could take some pride in."

MRS. MADISON (Reference librarian): "Miss Warren, I think that I ought to chime in at this point, just to give Frank a chance to catch his breath. When he told me on Wednesday what he had done about the telephone calls the previous evening, I agreed to let him try it again on Thursday. Without saying anything to him, or for that matter to anyone, I have tried the same thing myself for the last three evenings that I have been on duty, and the results have been phenomenal. For the first time in months, it's a pleasure for me to come to work in the evenings. Like Frank, I really feel that I'm accomplishing something, instead of rushing around like a slave to the silly phone. Now that we've tried this out, I'd like to ask your permission for us to do it all the time, and to just say, categorically, no more telephone reference questions from children."

MISS WARREN: "Well now, I would want to think this over before saying 'yes' to anything quite so drastic. I wonder what the rest of you think about all of this?"

MRS. TEMPLE (Children's librarian): I must say I agree with Miss Warren, this does sound quite drastic indeed. I don't quite see why the children should be discriminated against in this way—why they shouldn't be entitled to the same services that adults get? Why, we answer these questions on the telephone during the daytime in the children's room, and I've never felt that it was burdensome."

MR. SHERMAN: "But, that's just the point, Mrs. Temple. Do you get forty or fifty calls an afternoon in the children's room?"

MRS. TEMPLE: "Oh, I certainly wouldn't think so. Half a dozen, perhaps."

MR. SHERMAN: "That's exactly it. It's only in the evenings that this becomes a problem. Now, the other thing that I think it's important to point out is this: out of the thirty or so phone calls we got from these youngsters the other evening, I doubt that there was one that would legitimately qualify as a real reference question."

MISS WARREN: "How do you mean, Mr. Sherman? What are these calls like?"

MR. SHERMAN: "Most of them come from children in junior and senior high school—I would say the seventh and eighth graders are the worst offenders, although judging from some of the questions asked, I think this may be beginning to percolate down even to the elementary school level. There are questions on how to spell things, those are the most common, and, of course, could be answered by just consulting a dictionary. I suppose a few of these youngsters may not have a dictionary at home, or may not know how to use one, but my guess is that most of them are just too lazy to look the word up at home—it's easier to call the library. Then, there are questions about whether or not the library owns a certain book, and if so, whether or not the book's on the shelves. We might get fifteen calls a night, asking about the same book. Things like that, simple enough individually, but forty or fifty of them in a night can eat up an enormous amount of time. And what bothers me most is that it's time spent in an unproductive way."

MISS LUFKIN (Adult services librarian): "Mr. Sherman, don't you often have to answer the same kinds of questions for adults?"

MR. SHERMAN: "Yes, we often do."

MISS LUFKIN: "And do you consider it 'unproductive' when an adult asks a question like that?"

MR. SHERMAN: "No, I think that's quite a different matter."

MRS. MADISON: "Perhaps I can answer that, Miss Lufkin, and also come back to the question that Mrs. Temple raised when she was concerned about our 'discriminating' against children. The answer is that we *do* discriminate in our reference service to children all the time, and we do it quite deliberately. When children and teen-agers come into the library with simple questions like those Mr. Sherman mentioned, we do not find answers for them; we show the child how to look up the answer himself. We do this because we are trying to train these children to be able to use a library intelligently, because we feel that this is an obligation on our part, to teach children and young people how to use a dictionary, or how to look something up in the card catalog. I might add that the schools are very much in favor of our doing this. Mr. Sherman's point is that by using the telephone, these children are forcing us to do work for them that we would not do if they came to the library in person."

MISS LUFKIN: "I still think that your solution is a terribly negative one, and I'm concerned about the child who may have a legitimate need for information. Don't forget that these youngsters are our adult borrowers of the future. I have found that one of the great problems in getting adults to use the library is to overcome negative attitudes about the library that were formed by childhood experiences."

MR. SHERMAN: "I think that's a very idealistic theory, and I agree with it, *in theory*. But, the hard, cold facts are that it just doesn't work out in practice. I can understand how you might not see our problem, though. Mrs. Madison and I are each on duty at the reference desk two evenings a week. You are on duty at the desk only one evening a week, on Fridays, and Friday is the quietest evening of the whole week. You ought to try it on a Monday or Tuesday night, sometime, and then I think you'd understand a little better what we're talking about."

MISS WARREN: "I really think that we all *do* understand the problem that Mrs. Madison and Mr. Sherman are up against, and it is a difficult one. This is, of course, the perennial difficulty with telephone reference service: first, that the telephoner invariably takes precedence over the individual who has taken the trouble to come to the library in person; and secondly, that you find yourself doing things for the person who phones, that the person really ought to be going for himself, and would have to do for himself, if he came to the library in person. I will have to admit that I don't especially care for the picture Mr. Sherman has painted of an adult patron, and a taxpayer, being made to stand and wait for the benefit of some teen-aged lout lounging at the other end of the telephone line."

MR. SHERMAN: "That's just about what it amounts to, Miss Warren. And don't think for a minute these kids aren't smart enough to know it. Why, they're making fools of us."

MISS WARREN: "What you two are proposing, then, is that we refuse to provide telephone reference service, unless the caller is clearly identifiable as an adult, is that it?"

MRS. MADISON: "Well, certainly during the busy hours. I would say from the time school gets out in the afternoon until the evening closing hour. And, of course, all day on Saturday."

MISS WARREN: "I don't really think we could do it that way. I think it will have to be all or nothing. Anything else is just too confusing."

MRS. MADISON: "Then, I would have to say no telephone reference service to children at all."

MISS WARREN: "Does anyone have an alternate suggestion to make?"

MISS LUFKIN: "I suppose the obvious one is more staff. Is there any way that we could have two people on duty in the reference room, I mean two librarians, on these busy evenings? Then, one person could take care of the phone."

MISS DARBY (Assistant librarian): "Not a chance, I'm afraid. I can tell you, from making out the work schedules, that we're spread far too thin now. Unless, of course, we could add one or two more people."

MISS WARREN: "That, I can assure you, is completely out of the question, at least for the next two years. I have an absolute mandate from the mayor and the city council that there is to be no increase in the size of the staff this year or next."

MRS. MADISON: "I wonder, though, if we might not use our existing staff in a slightly different way? I hesitate to suggest this, because it is going to sound like a criticism of Miss Lufkin, and I want to make it clear that this is not what I mean at all. Please understand, Ruth, that I don't mean this personally, and that I do appreciate the importance of the work you're doing. But, the fact remains that the rest of us are scheduled right up to the hilt, while you are scheduled for desk duty only eight hours a week in total. That leaves 27 hours a week of your time for adult book selection, taking care of the films and phonograph records, the great books and golden age groups, and of course, your outside work with programing for clubs and organizations. I'm sure these jobs require all of that time and more, and I know for a fact that you often put in a work week that's closer to 60 hours than to 35. The question I'm asking, though, is whether this library can afford to devote 27 hours a week of professional staff time to these activities at this particular juncture, at a time when we are being pressed so hard in the reference area? For example, on the very evening that Frank was so terribly busy at the reference desk last week, you were conducting a film program right upstairs in the auditorium. I understand you had 45 adults there, and I'm sure many of them are people who would probably never have come into the library except to see a travel film on Italy. But, I took a look just before this meeting at the circulation figures for last Tuesday evening, and I find no substantial increase in the number of books borrowed. Now, in all honesty, isn't it true that most of the people who come to the library for these programs of yours never borrow a book, and, in all probability, never will borrow a book?"

MISS WARREN: "I don't think I am going to let Miss Lufkin answer that question, because I don't want anybody to feel they are on the defensive here. The adult services and programing were instituted here because I wanted them, and if that decision was a mistake, then it was my mistake and not Miss Lufkin's."

MRS. MADISON: "Let me make myself clear. When you decided to establish Miss Lufkin's position, and to go into this film and phonograph record activity in a substantial way, I was very much in favor of the idea, and I'm sure all of us in this room who were on the staff at the time were. But, I think things have changed in the last four years. Use of the library, and especially use of the reference room by students is far greater now than it was then; far greater than I would ever have imagined possible. I just wonder if first things don't have to come first, and if so, then shouldn't you reconsider the amount of time that is being invested in audio-visual services and group activities?"

MISS WARREN: "You are asking if we can afford to devote 27 hours a week of staff time to these adult and group activities. My reply would be to answer your question with a question: Can we afford *not* to? You know the kind of community this is as well as I do. We have never had, nor are we going to have in the future, a very high level of adult use here. Only a fraction of the adults in this community are real 'readers' in the usual sense of that word. Yet, all the adults in the community, in one way or another, have to pay the bill for the operation of this library, which is financed far better than even our public schools are. I think, and the trustees think, it is vital that we find a way to bring a larger segment of the adult population into contact with the library. Now, it is clear that conventional methods are not the answer here. That is why we created the post of adult services librarian, to have a person who would go out into the community in a dynamic way to show these people, who are non-readers, that the library is for them, too. In my personal opinion, this has paid off handsomely as a public relations venture, and I simply think it would be folly to cut back on our services in this area."

MRS. TEMPLE: "I agree. That is no solution. I doubt that we are going to come up with anything that is more attractive than what Mrs. Madison and Mr. Sherman have proposed. I would like to ask one question, though. Did I understand you to say that the people at the main circulation desk, some of whom are merely high school girls, are going to screen the telephone calls, and decide who gets connected with the reference desk, and who doesn't?"

MRS. MADISON: "Well, it would be the person at the circulation desk who happens to answer the telephone. This is usually one of the senior clerks on duty, but I will grant you that it is possible that the telephone could be answered by a student aide."

MRS. TEMPLE: "I think it is terribly dangerous for an untrained, inexperienced youngster to have that sort of responsibility. I would much rather have the reference librarian on duty do it, but then I suppose that would defeat the whole purpose of the scheme, wouldn't it?"

At this point, seeing that the noon hour was near, Miss Warren brought the meeting to a close. As Mrs. Madison was leaving, Miss Warren indicated that she and Mr. Sherman might, for the time being, continue to limit telephone reference service to adults, on a sort of temporary, emergency basis. Miss Warren made it clear, however, that she wished to give the matter further thought before making the new policy a permanent one.

How do you evaluate the several alternatives proposed by various members of the staff of the A_____ Public Library as a means of reducing pressures on the reference staff during evening hours? Are there other solutions, beyond those discussed during the staff meeting, that you consider more attractive than the elimination of telephone reference service to children? If Miss Warren asked your advice, would you recommend that telephone service be restricted to adults as Mrs. Madison and Mr. Sherman have proposed?

Did either Mr. Sherman or Mrs. Madison exceed their authority in deciding to impose restrictions on telephone reference service without having first consulted Miss Warren?

If children are to be denied reference service by telephone, what kinds of problems may be expected to arise, and how should Miss Warren and her staff plan to deal with them? How would you expect trustees, school officials, and the general public to respond to this new policy? Do you anticipate that a decision to restrict telephone service in this way might create public relations problems for the A_____ Public Library?

18 Selection of a Dictionary

Frances Ashburn is librarian of M____ Central Regional High School, located in the midst of a group of suburban communities on the outer fringe of a large city. The school has an enrollment of nearly 2,000 students in grades 9 through 12, and serves both the community of M____, in which it is located, and a half dozen smaller towns that do not have a sufficiently large student population to justify having their own high schools. Approximately 35 per cent of the graduates of M____ Central Regional High School go on to further education, while the remainder find employment in local businesses or on farms in the region.

The regional high school is a new one, now in its third year of operation. Its faculty is slightly above average in competence, although it has a somewhat smaller number of male teachers than one would usually find in a school this size. This is perhaps due to the fact that teachers' salaries at M____ are not especially high, so that male teachers who do come there are likely to move on, after a few years, to the urban high schools where salaries are more attractive.

The high school library is a good one, and is considered by many a model that might well be emulated by other communities in the area. Miss Ashburn joined the staff almost a year before the school opened and, working in rented quarters in a nearby office building, was able to select and organize a basic collection of nearly 6,000 titles before classes began in the new building. Since then, funds have been provided each year for the purchase of approximately 1,200 titles, so that the collection now numbers nearly 10,000 volumes in total. In general, the books have been well chosen, with a careful eye to the instructional program of the school and to standard lists of recommended titles for high school libraries. Miss Ashburn is also fortunate enough to have the services of a half-time clerical assistant, in addition to the usual corps of student aides, so that she has been able to devote a good deal of time to working with the faculty in integrating library assignments into classroom work in several subject areas, and to the reading guidance of individual students.

The principal of M_____ Central Regional High School is Edward Buhl. Mr. Buhl is a man in his mid-forties who has had almost ten years' experience as a secondary school administrator, including four and one-half years in his present post. He is an intelligent, able person who has a reputation for being fair-minded and honest, although somewhat humorless and lacking in imagination. Up to this point, his relationships with the school library and with Miss Ashburn have been quite harmonious.

One morning, as Miss Ashburn was working at her desk, she received a note from the principal, asking if she could meet with him in his office at the close of the school day, and if she would bring with her a list of the English language dictionaries in the school library collection. She replied in the affirmative, and set about preparing the list, which turned out not to be an especially lengthy one. It included *Webster's New International Dictionary of the English Language* (3d ed., unabridged), *Funk and Wagnall's New Standard Dictionary*, the *Oxford English Dictionary*, Craigie and Hulbert's *Dictionary of American English*, *Webster's New Collegiate Dictionary*, the *American College Dictionary*, Fowler's *Dictionary of Modern English Usage*, Mencken's *The American Language*, Partridge's *Dictionary of Slang*, Wentworth and Flexner's *Dictionary of American Slang* and *Webster's Dictionary of Synonyms*. With this list in hand, Miss Ashburn appeared in Mr. Buhl's office at the appointed hour.

"Miss Ashburn, I do appreciate your being willing to meet with me on such short notice this afternoon. I wonder if you have brought along the dictionary list I asked for?"

"Yes, I have brought it."

She handed the list to Mr. Buhl, who looked at it for a moment and then said: "Ah, yes. This is the book I'm interested in, and wanted to talk with you about, the *Dictionary of American Slang*."

"Wentworth and Flexner?"

"Yes. Do you happen, by any chance, to remember why we purchased this dictionary?"

"I'm not quite sure I understand your question, Mr. Buhl. You want to know *why* we bought Wentworth and Flexner?"

"Let me put the question another way. Did some teacher ask to have this book added to our library?"

"Why, I really can't recall offhand. I know that we've had the book for some time."

"How long, can you recall?"

"Oh, a couple of years, at least. Mr. Buhl, do you have time for me to run down to the library and check my records? I keep a file for every book we order, indicating on whose recommendation it was purchased. It wouldn't take a minute for me to look this book up."

"Why, yes, if you wouldn't mind doing that. By the way, do you happen to know if the book is in at the moment?"

"I'm sure it is. It's a reference book, so that it can't be taken from the library."

"If you don't mind, would you bring it along with you when you're coming?"

Miss Ashburn excused herself, and re-appeared in Mr. Buhl's office a few moments later with the book and a copy of the original order for it.

"Here is the book. Now, this is the original request for it. We've had the book for three years; it was among the first group we bought for the library. I see from this record that I selected it myself. No one on the faculty asked for it."

"I see. I thought perhaps some one of our former teachers might have requested it." Mr. Buhl paused and then continued, "Before you came down to the office today, I did check with the English department, through the chairman, and apparently none of the people up there were even aware we had this book."

"Mr. Buhl, you speak as though there were something wrong with the book."

"Are you familiar with its contents?"

"Why, yes, in a general way. I know that it's a dictionary of current American slang usage, and that it's intended to serve as a supplement to the general English language dictionaries, which don't include slang."

"Have you ever looked at it closely, I mean from the point of view of content?" Mr. Buhl asked.

"Well, to be honest, I haven't often had occasion to use it in reference work."

"To be perfectly candid with you, Miss Ashburn, I learned today, quite by chance, that this book contains a substantial number of obscene terms, complete with definitions. Apparently, some of our youngsters have discovered this, and the book has pretty much become the talk of the school. Notes are being circulated among students, citing the page numbers where these four-letter words may be found. One of the notes found its way to my desk, and that's how I discovered it."

At that point, Mr. Buhl took a slip of paper on which some page numbers were apparently written, and began to examine pages in the dictionary, which lay open before him. After a few minutes, he said: "Miss Ashburn, this is really pretty raw stuff. I'm a reasonably liberal person, but, frankly, I find this extreme. I'm not going to embarrass you by asking you to look at these definitions, but take my word for it, these are four-letter words in the literal sense of that term. I just can't understand *how* we could ever have bought a book like this."

"I'll take your word for the contents, Mr. Buhl, although I am a bit surprised, and I must say I hadn't realized it was such strong stuff. As I said, I have not had much occasion to use the book, it's just been sitting on the shelves since we bought it. I do remember, though, that the reviews of it were excellent at the time it was published." Miss Ashburn continued, "In fact, if I'm not mistaken, it had a feature review in the *New York Times*. And, I'm sure it appears on standard lists of recommended reference books, which is probably why we bought it in the first place."

"Well, I certainly don't think we can leave it sitting on the shelves any longer, do you?"

"I don't know . . ."

"Look, Miss Ashburn, I detest anything that smacks of censorship or book burning just as much as the next person. You know that I've never interfered in the slightest with the books you've bought for the school library, in all of the time we've been working together. Isn't that right?"

"Yes, you've been wonderful in that respect. I've always felt you were very broad–minded and liberal in your attitude towards the library. By the same token," Miss Ashburn explained, "I have tried to be reasonably discreet in selecting books, although I do feel that we have an obligation to provide some reading at the adult level for our more able boys and girls."

"I quite agree," said Mr. Buhl. "Now, I know that you have books in the school library that some people might find fault with. Things like *Catcher in the Rye* and *Andersonville*. I would absolutely defend, and I have defended, without your ever knowing it, our right, in fact our obligation, to provide books of that sort for the more serious students who can handle them. I'm glad these books are available to our students, and I want to keep it that way. But, to my mind, this is quite a different matter."

"In the first place," Buhl continued, "it's a reference book, and I don't think we can justify having a book in our reference library unless it is directly related to our teaching program. This is not supplementary or optional reading in the way that a novel might be. As far as I can see, after checking with the faculty, this book does not serve to further our instructional program in any way. If I were called upon to defend it, to explain to a parent or to a member of the school board why we have it, I don't think I could. I just don't believe this book belongs in a high school library. I think that in a college it would be perfectly all right, where the people using it would be mature enough to handle it. I think we probably ought not to have bought it for the library in the first place. Since it was purchased over my signature, and I'm responsible for it, I am going to ask you to remove it from the shelves."

"The only thing is, if the students are all talking about it, isn't taking it off the shelves just going to arouse their curiosity even more?" Miss Ashburn asked.

"I think that's probably true, but I believe it's far more dangerous to leave it on the shelves," said Mr. Buhl. "Incidentally, I should appreciate having the name of any boy or girl who asks for the book after you've removed it."

If you were Miss Ashburn, would you agree to the removal of the *Dictionary of American Slang* from the shelves of the school library? Do you agree with Mr. Buhl that this book is not appropriate for the reference collection of a high school library, and ought not to have been purchased in the first place? How might Miss Ashburn defend her purchase of the book?

Do you feel that different standards must be applied in the selection of books for the reference collection in a school library than are employed in choosing the general book collection? Specifically, should the reference collection in a library of this kind be restricted to books that are requested by the faculty or are directly related to the instructional program of the school?

19 The Longest Filibuster

"Miss Vernon, I wonder if you remember me, Harry Stamford, at the *Clarion-News*?" Alice Vernon, Chief of the Reference Department of the W_____ Public Library, had just responded to the ringing telephone on her desk, and her caller had identified himself. "Yes, Mr. Stamford," Miss Vernon replied, "I certainly do remember you, although I must admit that I had to stop and think for a minute. It's been quite a while since you and I have talked."

MR. STAMFORD: "Yes, last spring, if my memory serves me correctly."

MISS VERNON: "That's right. It was when you did the story for National Library Week. That was an excellent story, by the way. All of us on the staff were so pleased with it."

MR. STAMFORD: "That's very nice to hear. You have a fine library, and we were glad to have a chance to tell people about it. Now, I'm afraid it's my turn to ask you for some help."

MISS VERNON: "Why, of course. What can we do for you?"

MR. STAMFORD: "Miss Vernon, you may remember that I am responsible for our Sunday editorial and feature supplement. To get right to the point, I'm putting together a feature story, for this Sunday's edition, on Congress, specifically, on that curious Congressional phenomenon known as the *filibuster*. I'm facing a deadline at five o'clock this afternoon, and I need a couple of facts. Usually, I do my own research, but I'm really pressed today and so I thought that with all those research questions you are always answering, perhaps you wouldn't mind one more."

MISS VERNON: "Certainly. What do you need?"

MR. STAMFORD: "Two things. First, I'd like a few examples of what goes into filibuster speeches. I know that they are filled with all sorts of meaningless material, because the purpose of them is just to kill time. But, I've never seen any actual examples of the kinds of things that are said by a speaker during a filibuster, have you?"

MISS VERNON: "Now that you mention it, I don't believe I have either. Like you, I have a general idea of what they consist of, but I've never seen exactly what is said."

MR. STAMFORD: "Do you think you could find some examples for me?"

MISS VERNON: "I think so. We have almost a complete set of the *Congressional Record,* ever since it began. That's a record of everything that's said in Congress, and it ought to be easy enough to look back and find some controversial bill that provoked a filibuster for an example or two of a filibuster speech."

MR. STAMFORD: "That would be splendid. You also have a machine in your department for photostating printed pages, don't you?"

MISS VERNON: "Yes, we have a rapid copier. It would be quite simple to photocopy some pages from the *Congressional Record.*"

MR. STAMFORD: "Fine. I'd be glad to pay the charge for that, of course."

MISS VERNON: "Well, if we've solved that problem, what was the other thing you wanted?"

MR. STAMFORD: "This sounds more difficult, although it will probably be no problem at all for you. I'd like to find out what the longest filibuster on record was, in the history of Congress. I'd like to know what it was about, who the major participants were, and how it all came out. Some samples from the speeches made at that time would be awfully useful too, if those were available."

MISS VERNON: "We'll be glad to try and see what we can locate. How soon do you need to have this?"

MR. STAMFORD: "Well, as I said, my deadline, unfortunately, is five o'clock today. Let me see, it's nine-thirty now. I could probably get over to the library right after lunch, at say, two o'clock. That would give me time to look at anything you've been able to find, pick up the photostats, and get back to my desk by three to finish my copy. Would that be all right with you?"

MISS VERNON: "All right. We'll look for you at two o'clock. Come to the reference desk in the main reading room, and I'll be there."

MR. STAMFORD: "Fine, I'll see you then. And, thank you, Miss Vernon, I'll be very grateful for any help you can give me."

The W⸺ Public Library is one of the strongest libraries in the region in which it is located. It serves the city of W⸺ which, with its population of 400,000, is the largest in the state, although not the state capital. The library houses almost a quarter of a million volumes.

The general reference collection is a good one, and contains most of the fact-finding titles listed in the latest edition of the Enoch Pratt Free Library's *Reference Books*, which has been used by Miss Vernon as a buying guide. The collection is less complete in bibliographical reference sources. For example, the library owns only *Evans*, the *United States Catalog* and the *Cumulative Book Index* among the retrospective American national and trade bibliographies. Similarly, the library lacks several of the specialized indexes to periodicals such as *Applied Science and Technology Index*.

The W_____ Public Library has been a partial depository for United States government documents since 1895. Holdings include most of the twentieth century volumes of the serial set, as well as a fairly complete file, at least since the 1890's, of the *Congressional Record*. In general, the collection of late nineteenth and twentieth century Congressional documents is quite complete, and, of course, the library also has the general indexes to federal documents.

Indicate in detail how you would go about finding the material Mr. Stamford has asked for, with full citations showing the location of the desired information. It should be borne in mind that time is a factor here, so that the search should be organized and carried out in an especially expeditious manner.

Is it possible to locate this material in the amount of time available to Miss Vernon? Can she be criticized in any way for her handling of the reference interview?

20 A Doctoral Dissertation

J——— College is a small, privately-supported, liberal arts institution for men located in a suburb of a large eastern city. Both the college as a whole, and the college library, might best be described by the word "average." J——— has, for more than 100 years, offered the traditional four years of liberal arts and sciences, with the conventional majors, to its 800 undergraduate men. The faculty, although competent, is not especially distinguished. The same mediocrity extends to the student body, so that academic standards do not tend to be particularly high. The general climate of the college is one of calm deliberation, with little stimulus for change or experiment in teaching, and virtually no faculty research.

Under such circumstances, it is not surprising to find that the college library has developed along rather conventional lines. It is housed in an alumni memorial building constructed in 1925, featuring an imposing neo-Georgian façade, and an interior characterized by large, "railway-waiting-room style," reading rooms, closed stacks, oak furniture and rather drab, institutional colors. The book collection has gradually increased in size, if not in quality, over the years, so that it now numbers some 150,000 volumes, a figure which is very near the book capacity of the present building.

The library has a staff of 15 full-time employees, plus the usual number of part-time student assistants. The professional staff of seven includes two catalogers, an acquisitions librarian, a circulation librarian, a periodicals librarian, a reference librarian, and the library director, Dr. Anson. Dr. Anson is 57 years old, and holds a Ph.D. in history. He has had no formal training in librarianship. He has directed the library for the past eight years, during which time he has continued to hold the rank of Professor of History, teaching on a half-time basis in the history department. It is generally understood that his appointment as director of the library stemmed from a wish on the part of the President of J_____ to reward him for many years of faithful service to the college. He was in rather poor health at the time of his appointment to the directorship of the library, and this, coupled with a fairly heavy teaching load, has left little time for him to become involved in the operation of the library. He has interested himself mainly in acquisitions in the field of history, and in particular in the selection and purchase of materials relating to the Ante-Bellum South, his own area of specialization. All purchase recommendations in this area are handled by Dr. Anson personally, and he spends a good deal of time browsing in bookshops in the neighboring city, chatting with book dealers, and scanning booksellers' catalogs for desirable items. As a result, the library has developed a rather interesting collection of books, pamphlets, newspapers and memorabilia relating to the southern states before the Civil War. All of these items have been carefully cataloged by Dr. Anson, and many of them line the bookshelves in his office.

With the exceptions noted above, Dr. Anson has been content to leave the actual operation of the library to the supervision of the professional staff. As one might imagine, at a college like J_____, pressures on the library are not great, and, by and large, the ladies of the staff manage to keep things going quite smoothly. Dr. Anson presides over the entire operation with a kindly and benign paternalism and rarely interferes in the daily conduct of library affairs.

The only other male member of the library staff is Frank Torrington, the reference librarian. Mr. Torrington is 25 years old and has held his present position for five months. He has had no previous library experience. After graduating from J_____ College with an A.B. in English literature, Mr. Torrington entered the armed forces. Upon completion of his military service, he taught for one year in a junior high school and then enrolled in the graduate school of library science at a nearby university. Shortly thereafter, he accepted the post of reference librarian at J_____, and he now pursues his studies on a part-time basis. Mr. Torrington is a bright, alert young man who gives every evidence of genuine professional promise, and who is both ambitious and anxious to prove himself. As is the case with many young people, he is disarmingly frank and quick to criticize, and this has led on occasion to strained relationships with other members of the staff.

Quite early in his tenure at J_____, Mr. Torrington was disappointed to discover that the college library, and in particular the reference librarian, had little or no part in the instructional process. Indeed, the chief duties of the reference librarian were to maintain the reference room as a quiet study area, and to answer occasional directional questions. As most teaching was done through lectures, coupled with required readings in reserve books, there was little need for students to carry on the kind of independent investigation and study that necessitates the use of reference materials. Neither students nor faculty seemed to have a sense of the library as an informational resource, nor had the library in the past ever consciously sought to develop such an image.

Mr. Torrington felt that this was an unhappy state of affairs, and he resolved to attempt to bring the library actively into the teaching program. He set up a series of lectures and informal tours for freshmen and prepared, with Dr. Anson's approval, a mimeographed guide to the library to be distributed during the college registration period. These ventures met with some modest success, although it is safe to say that they were hardly noticed by faculty and students in general. Nevertheless, there were a few younger people on the faculty who seemed sympathetic with what Mr. Torrington was trying to do, and who even suggested that, at some future time, he might perhaps be invited to work with their students when assignments involving research were made. Mr. Torrington assiduously pursued these contacts, in the hope that one or more of them might materialize during the forthcoming Spring semester. He felt that if he could wangle one or two invitations to work with smaller, advanced classes, he could demonstrate convincingly the values of intelligent use of reference materials, in terms of student work of improved quality.

One morning, late in the fall, as Mr. Torrington was drinking a cup of coffee in the college snack bar, he was joined by Bertram Marshall, a young man who had recently been appointed Assistant Professor of Psychology, and who was in his first year of teaching at J_____. The two men had met a number of times and had had lunch together on one or two occasions in the college dining room. They chatted amiably for a few minutes, and just as Mr. Torrington was about to excuse himself to return to his desk in the library, Mr. Marshall said: "Say, you know, I've been thinking about you. I'm going to be working with the seniors in the psychology research seminar next semester, since Jim Norton will be on sabbatical. I've been wondering if there's some way that we might get them to use the library more, do some real digging into journals and that sort of thing."

MR. TORRINGTON: "Well, I'd be all for that, of course."

MR. MARSHALL: "I'm afraid the problem for most of them would be that they wouldn't know how to begin. Of course, I know research method, but I wish I knew more about our own library. Actually, I do most of my own research at L_____, in the city."

MR. TORRINGTON: "Perhaps there's some way that I could be helpful."

MR. MARSHALL: "Actually, that's just what I was thinking. You know, the other day at lunch you were saying something about library orientation. Maybe I could bring the class over to the library one day, and you could sort of show them around."

MR. TORRINGTON: "Yes, I'd be glad to do that. Or, you might prefer to have me meet with the class first. I could bring some samples of various reference books with me, and explain them. Of course, I wouldn't presume to discuss the reference literature of your own field. You would be the only person qualified to do that. But, I do think there might be things like, for example, the *Union List of Serials,* that are outside of your own field, but are very useful in research."

MR. MARSHALL: "*Union List of Serials?* I don't believe that I've ever used that."

MR. TORRINGTON: "You know, it's a list of periodicals. Shows where back files are located in libraries."

MR. MARSHALL: "What do you know! Is this *Union List* thing something we have in our library?"

MR. TORRINGTON: "Sure."

MR. MARSHALL: "I'd like to see that sometime, myself. Of course, I don't know how useful it would be in the kind of research our students would be doing. Still, I suppose it wouldn't do any harm for them to know about it. I'll tell you what. Are you going back to the library now?"

MR. TORRINGTON: "Yes, I am."

MR. MARSHALL: "If you don't mind, I'll walk along with you."

The two men walked back to the library together, and on the way, set a date for Mr. Torrington to meet with Mr. Marshall's seminar group early in the following semester. Mr. Torrington was delighted at the opportunity, as it represented the first invitation of this kind that he had had from a member of the faculty. He spoke with considerable animation of the kinds of reference materials that might be brought to the attention of Mr. Marshall's students, and Mr. Marshall seemed to respond with equal enthusiasm to his every suggestion. As they reached the corridor outside the reference room, Mr. Marshall said: "You know, this kind of thing that you're trying to do is really great for students. In fact, I don't mind confessing that I'll probably learn a good deal from your talk myself. I sort of envy the students, getting this help."

MR. TORRINGTON: "Well, you know, the library can help the faculty with research too. That's what we're here for."

MR. MARSHALL: "You mean, looking up references, and that sort of thing?"

MR. TORRINGTON: "Why certainly, Mr. Marshall."

MR. MARSHALL: "Call me Bert, won't you, Frank? After all, we're going to be working together."

MR. TORRINGTON: "OK, Bert."

MR. MARSHALL: "Say, Frank. Do you have just another minute?"

MR. TORRINGTON: "Yes."

MR. MARSHALL: "I was just wondering. I don't suppose you could look up some references for me, could you?"

MR. TORRINGTON: "Sure! I'd be glad to."

MR. MARSHALL: "What I need are some references on testing."

MR. TORRINGTON: "Do you mean books on testing?"

MR. MARSHALL: "No, not exactly. What I'm after is more in test analysis, if you see what I'm getting at."

MR. TORRINGTON: "I'm not sure I do. I'm afraid I don't know much about testing."

MR. MARSHALL: "Did you ever hear of the Strong Vocational Preference Test?"

MR. TORRINGTON: "Oh, sure!"

MR. MARSHALL: "Well, that's the test I've been working on. In fact, I've been devoting myself for the past two years to giving the Strong Test to college freshmen. I'm doing an evaluation of the test as my dissertation. I can tell you, it's a relief to have it all finished and written up."

MR. TORRINGTON: "You've completed the dissertation?"

MR. MARSHALL: "Just about. It's all written up and I'm in the process of having it typed. Oh, I'm still putting some of the statistics together, but the big problem at the moment is a bibliography. I'll have to have one, and frankly, I don't see how I can get it together, and still make the January deadline. I have to have the dissertation completed by the 6th, if I want to get the degree in February."

MR. TORRINGTON: "Didn't you compile a bibliography when you began the research?"

MR. MARSHALL: "Frank, I never thought about it. It was strictly field research, you see. Original, experimental work. Even if I'd had the time, which I didn't, there wouldn't have been any point. But, my thesis committee will expect a bibliography, and I suppose they'll expect a fairly complete one. That's why I thought, if it wouldn't be too much trouble, perhaps you could get together some references on testing and test evaluation for me. From what you've been saying, I would think that for you this wouldn't take too much time, would it?"

MR. TORRINGTON: "No, it really wouldn't."

MR. MARSHALL: "That would be great, Frank. I'd really appreciate it. Say, I have to get to class. Could you give me a ring tomorrow or the next day, if you're able to find anything?"

MR. TORRINGTON: "I certainly will. Don't worry, I think I can find plenty of material for you. Will you want to see the books and periodicals, or do you just want the citations?"

MR. MARSHALL: "Just the references will be fine. I really have to go now. Thanks, again."

Mr. Torrington was extremely pleased with the results of his conversation with Mr. Marshall. Not only was he grateful for the invitation to participate in Mr. Marshall's seminar, but he was equally happy to have an opportunity to demonstrate his abilities as a bibliographer to a member of the faculty. Moreover, he found the prospect of compiling this bibliography interesting, especially in comparison to the usual routine of handling simple directional questions at the reference desk. He set to work immediately to compile a suitable list of books and periodical articles, and devoted the remainder of the day, as well as the day following, to its preparation. Late the following afternoon, he telephoned Mr. Marshall who came to the library to pick up a neatly typed list of some 50 books and periodical articles. Mr. Marshall was profuse in expressing his appreciation, and quite flattering in commenting on Mr. Torrington's ability to locate information on a difficult topic.

Had you been in Mr. Torrington's place, how would you have responded to Mr. Marshall's request for a thesis bibliography? How do you evaluate Mr. Torrington's response to this request, as this is described in this case?

21 The Cost of Living

The C_____ Public Library serves an industrial and residential community of 74,000 through a central library and four branches. The largest of the branch libraries has a book collection of approximately 7,500 volumes, half of which are juvenile titles. This branch is located near a large junior-senior high school, and is approximately six miles away from the central library. The nearby school has a few books obtained through the classroom deposit service of the public library, but no library of its own, and, of course, no school librarian. Accordingly, the public library branch is heavily used by children and young people, especially during the afternoon and evening hours.

The branch is staffed by a single professionally trained librarian, Miss Bisbee, who has the title of branch librarian. She is assisted by one full-time clerical person, and a number of high school girls who work at the circulation desk during the busy after-school periods. Miss Bisbee's desk is located just behind the circulation desk, in a public area, and she provides such reference assistance as is needed by those who use the branch.

The C_____ Public Library is, generally speaking, neither especially well supported nor very ably administered, and its collections and services are best described as "average" for a public library its size in a community that is neither prosperous nor "library-minded." The branch libraries are primarily a source for recreational reading, so that the adult book collection in Miss Bisbee's branch, consisting of perhaps 3,500 titles, is comprised largely of popular non-fiction (books on home decoration, gardening, hobbies, and the like), mysteries, westerns, light novels, and multiple copies of current best sellers. The funds allocated for branch library book purchases are quite modest, and Miss Bisbee finds that there is very little money left for the acquisition of more substantial books after the demands for recreational reading have been met.

No particular effort has been made to build up the reference collection in the branch, and it consists largely of older reference works transferred there, as these have been replaced by newer editions at the central library. Comparatively few reference books are purchased directly for branch use, since the administration of the library prefers to concentrate reference resources at the central library, on the theory that the branches are primarily book distribution centers, and, accordingly, require little in the way of reference materials. This theory is, in fact, rather well borne out in practice, and most people who need to use reference books or to obtain reference assistance tend, quite naturally, to go to the central library. Indeed, most of the "reference questions" that Miss Bisbee deals with in the course of a typical day in her branch library are either simple directional questions or requests for assistance that are most properly described as "readers advisory" services.

The few reference books that the branch does have are comparatively little used. These include:

A set of the *Cumulative Book Index,* covering the period from 1952 to the present.

A set of the *Abridged Reader's Guide to Periodical Literature,* covering the period from 1949 to the present.

Encyclopedia Americana (6 years old)

Collier's Encyclopedia (12 years old)

World Book Encyclopedia (2 years old)

Encyclopaedia Britannica (8 years old) plus the *Britannica Book of the Year,* 1950 to the present.

Statesman's Yearbook (8 years old)

Political Handbook of the World (2 years old)

World Almanac (the current edition has been stolen from the shelves, and only a 1951 edition is available)

Statistical Abstract of the United States (latest edition)

Historical Statistics of the United States (1949 edition with 1952 supplement)

Economic Almanac (7 years old)

Facts on File (current subscription)

The usual dictionaries, biographical sources and a few subject handbooks round out the branch reference collection. There is a small pamphlet file, consisting of six file drawers of material, but this has never been weeded, and contains few recent pamphlets. Additions to the pamphlet file come chiefly from unsolicited free material, articles and pictures cut from old magazines that are to be discarded by the library, and the like.

One evening, while Miss Bisbee was covering the circulation desk during the dinner hour, a teen-aged boy came up to the desk, and said, "Can you help me find some books?"

"What sort of books are you looking for?"

"Have you got any books about foreign countries?"

"Yes, we have," said Miss Bisbee. "Is this for a school assignment?"

"Yes. I need something on Sweden."

"Have you looked in the card catalog?"

"Can't you tell me whether or not you have books about Sweden?"

"Well, I'm sure that we do, but, just offhand, I don't recall what they are. Why don't you look in the catalog over there under 'Sweden' and copy down the numbers on the cards for any that have that word at the top of the card in red. I have to answer this telephone now, but you come back when you've copied the numbers, and I'll show you where to find the books."

Miss Bisbee turned to answer the telephone, that had been ringing insistently, and then occupied herself with charging out books and the other business of the circulation desk. The boy returned a few minutes later with several call numbers noted on a slip of paper. Miss Bisbee directed him to the section of the shelves where the books were located, and turned to another library patron who was awaiting her assistance. In due course, her clerical assistant returned from the evening meal to take charge of the circulation desk and, about 15 minutes later, Miss Bisbee looked up to find the boy who had wanted books about Sweden standing in front of her desk, holding four books in his hand. "Haven't you got anything newer than these?"

"Don't they have what you want?"

"No, they're no good—too old. I need something modern."

"Well, suppose we take a look at the card catalog again," said Miss Bisbee. "By the way, it might help if I knew exactly what you were looking for—is it some particular information about Sweden that you want, or is it just general?"

"Just general, I guess. Some stuff for school."

"What kind of stuff?"

"Figures. Hey, have you got any books with figures in them?" the boy asked.

"Figures?"

"You know, figures about Sweden."

"Do you mean statistics?"

"I guess so. I'm supposed to get these figures about Sweden—about the cost of living there and here."

"You mean that you want a comparison of the cost of living in Sweden with the cost of living in this country?"

"Yeah, that's what she—I mean, the teacher—said we should get. Most of the kids gave theirs today, you know, for other countries. So I've got to have the ones for Sweden tomorrow."

"You mean that the other people in the class had to get comparative statistics for other countries?" The boy nodded affirmatively, and Miss Bisbee said, "How did they get their statistics?"

"I don't know. I think maybe some of them went over to the big library, but I'm not sure."

"Well, you probably could do this more easily at the main library, in the reference room there. Why don't you go over there too?"

"I can't," said the boy, "I don't have a car."

Miss Bisbee nodded. Since there was no direct public transportation from the neighborhood in which her branch was located to the central library, she realized that there would be no way for him to get there without an automobile. By now, she had led the boy to the card catalog, and opening it to the entries under the subject heading "Sweden," she found five titles listed. Of the five, only one, *Sweden: the Welfare State* by Wilfrid Fleisher (John Day, 1956) had been published very recently.

"Did you find this book on the shelves?" she asked, pointing to the card for the Fleisher book. The boy said that he had not, and a quick check of the shelves showed that the book was indeed missing, and presumably charged out. Of the remaining four titles which the card catalog indicated dealt with Sweden, one was a book on Scandinavian furniture published in 1945, two were travel books published in the 1920's, and the fourth was a book on Swedish cooking. She next turned to the pamphlet file, but, as she had anticipated, found nothing in the folder on "Sweden" that was at all relevant to the problem at hand. The boy was clearly becoming restless, and Miss Bisbee suspected that he had already spent far more time in the library than he had expected to, and that he was about ready to give up on the assignment. She also realized that it was now 7:30 in the evening, that the library was beginning to fill up with adults and young people, and that she might have to limit the amount of time that she could give to the problem at hand.

What alternatives are open to Miss Bisbee at this point? Which of these is most likely to lead to a satisfactory resolution of the problem at hand in the shortest possible amount of time? Indicate specifically the steps to be taken in order to locate up-to-date comparative cost-of-living statistics for the United States and Sweden that will be adequate for the purposes of the school assignment. Is it possible to resolve this problem within the scope of the resources known to be available at the branch library? What would you do next, if you were Miss Bisbee?

22 Life
Expectancy

One afternoon, shortly after the end of the final class period of the day as Elizabeth Massena, librarian of L_____ High School, was busy gathering up library books from the study tables and returning them to the shelves, she was surprised to see Mrs. Fargo, a secretary in the office of the superintendent of schools, enter the library. Mrs. Fargo glanced around the room as though searching for something or someone, and then went to a range of shelves near the circulation desk where encyclopedias and other reference books were kept. Mrs. Fargo selected a volume of an encyclopedia, seated herself at a nearby table, and began to read. Assuming that her assistance was not needed, Miss Massena finished her housekeeping duties, arranged a few books on the shelves at the far end of the room, and began to prepare to close the library for the afternoon.

Some minutes later, after she had completed most of the customary closing hour routines, Miss Massena returned to the circulation desk, and noticed that Mrs. Fargo was still apparently engrossed in her reading. Miss Massena made a few rather obvious gestures to indicate that it was closing time, including turning off most of the reading room lights. Finally, Mrs. Fargo glanced up from her book, looked at the clock, and said: "My goodness, are you closing up?"

"Why, yes, Mrs. Fargo. We close at three," said Miss Massena.

"I see. I don't suppose that I could take this book down to my office, could I? We're there until five, and, of course, I could bring it back to you in the morning."

"Well, it is a reference book, and we don't usually let our encyclopedias go out of the library. Do you have very much more to do? Because if you don't, I'd prefer to wait and give you time to finish rather than to have you take the book out."

119

"All right, if you don't mind. I hope it won't take much longer. The only thing is, I'm expecting Mr. Franklin back from a meeting soon, and he'll wonder where I am."

"Since you won't be too much longer, why don't I just wait for a few minutes?"

Miss Massena went into her office, a glassed-in alcove just next to the reading room, and opened a recent issue of a book-reviewing periodical that had been lying on her desk for the past few days, awaiting her attention. She was a little annoyed at being forced to stay in the library beyond the usual closing hour, and she reflected somewhat bitterly to herself that neither Mrs. Fargo nor the other secretary in the super-intendent of schools' office were particularly noted for *their* amiability with members of the teaching staff of the high school. On the other hand, Mr. Franklin *was* the superintendent of schools, and, she sup-posed, one could hardly push his personal secretary out the library door.

A few minutes later, Mrs. Fargo appeared in the doorway of Miss Massena's office and announced: "You can close up now. It was a waste of time, anyway. Couldn't find what I wanted."

"That's too bad."

"Oh, I told Mr. Franklin that you probably wouldn't have it. But, he insisted that I come all the way up here anyway. He'll just have to do without it, that's all."

"Was it something important?"

"I haven't the faintest notion."

While this conversation was going on, Miss Massena had put on her coat, extinguished the remaining lights in the library, and locked the door, so that the two women were now in the corridor outside the library. As they walked down the corridor together Miss Massena said, "Well, perhaps you could come back to the library in the morning, or, maybe Mr. Franklin could stop in himself?" "Him? Go up to the library?" Mrs. Fargo responded. "You'll wait a long time if you're waiting to see that. Oh, no, he'd rather send someone else up there to waste their time for an hour. Well, here's my office."

Mrs. Fargo entered the office of the superintendent of schools, while Miss Massena continued on to the school parking area, got into her car, and drove off. She was still angry at being detained by Mrs. Fargo, and rather irritated that the older woman should describe going to the school library as "wasting time." She did a few errands at the downtown stores, and then drove home, arriving there shortly after 4:30 p.m. As she came down the hall towards her apartment, she could hear her tele-phone ringing. She hurried inside, lifted the receiver, and was surprised to hear an unfamiliar male voice at the other end:

"Miss Massena?"

"Yes."

"Miss Massena, this is Frederick Franklin. I'm dreadfully sorry to have to trouble you at home, but I need some assistance in rather a hurry, and it occurred to me that I might be able to prevail upon your good nature to help me out."

"Why certainly, Mr. Franklin. Was it something to do with the library?"

"Yes, it is. You see, I had asked my secretary to get some information for me from the library, while I was away at a meeting, during the early part of the afternoon. Apparently the library was closed or something, and, unfortunately, I gather you were not available. At any rate, I don't have the information and it occurred to me that since I'm at school, I could go up to the library and look it up myself, if only I knew where to find it."

"Mr. Franklin, would you want me to come over to school myself and help you?"

"I'm afraid there isn't time. The situation is this. I'm scheduled to be at a banquet about thirty minutes from now in honor of Mr. Denton. Do you know him?"

"No, I've never met Mr. Denton. I know who he is, of course."

"Then you also know that Mr. Denton has resigned as principal of the junior high school in order to accept a teaching post next year in the Philippines on one of the government exchange programs. His fellow teachers are holding a banquet in his honor this evening, and they've asked me to be their speaker, and to present a small gift to him. Mrs. Fargo is in the midst of typing my speech right now, and this is why I need your help. Let me explain that my remarks are intended to be both brief and rather light in tone, in keeping with the occasion, and I've tried to include a few humorous references to conditions in the Philippines as contrasted with conditions here in the U.S.A. Since I've travelled in the East myself, I know a good deal about conditions there, but I want, among other things, to compare life expectancy for men there with life expectancy here. I think the figure for the Philippines is something like 45 years as the average life expectancy for men, and this is where the humor comes in, because Mr. Denton just passed his 47th birthday. Now, to get to the point of my question, I wanted to know *exactly* what the current life expectancy for men in the Philippines is, and I wondered if there would be any book in the school library that I could go up and look in, while the rest of my speech is being typed? Would you know offhand where I might find that figure?"

Miss Massena thought for a moment or two, and then remembered that the school library did have a copy of the 1963 edition of the

Demographic Yearbook, issued by the United Nations, which she felt sure would contain life expectancy statistics for the Philippine Republic. She explained to Mr. Franklin where this book could be found on the school library reference shelves. He seemed delighted at her ability to suggest the proper source so readily, and indicated that he would go upstairs to the library at once. Mr. Franklin thanked Miss Massena for her assistance, apologized again for bothering her at home, and hung up.

Ten minutes later, as Miss Massena was beginning to prepare dinner in the kitchen of her small apartment, her telephone rang again. Upon responding, she recognized Mr. Franklin's voice, sounding rather harried, on the other end.

"Miss Massena, I *am* sorry to keep bothering you like this, but it seems that I'm in a blind alley here, and time is getting short. I'm up in the library right now, and I have this *Demographic Yearbook* open before me to page 620. The figure given for male life expectancy in the Philippines is 48.81 years, but this table indicates that the statistics are for 1946 to 1949. Don't we have any later statistics, or perhaps a later edition of this yearbook?"

"Mr. Franklin, are you sure you have the *Demographic Yearbook* for 1963, and not an earlier edition?"

"Yes, I'm quite sure that I have the edition for 1963, but apparently the figures in it are not up-to-date. Now, I've got just about ten minutes either to find an up-to-date life expectancy figure or else to try to re-cast my speech for tonight completely. What would you suggest I do?"

The L_____ High School library serves nearly 600 students and contains approximately 8,000 volumes, including some 350 titles on the reference shelves. The collection has been chosen to supplement the curriculum, with a few titles purchased each year for recreational reading. The library has an annual book budget of $1,100, about 10 percent of which goes for reference books. The reference book allocation provides for a subscription to the *Abridged Reader's Guide to Periodical Literature,* the replacement of a worn-out encyclopedia or unabridged dictionary every three or four years, and a few inexpensive reference works. The library subscribes to 30 current periodicals, most of them covered by the *Abridged Reader's Guide.*

L_____ is a small, semi-rural community, with no public library resources to speak of within the town, except for state-operated bookmobile service. The nearest large city is more than 50 miles away, and there are no colleges or universities in the immediate area.

Given these circumstances, if you were Miss Massena, what would you say or do at this point in the conversation with Mr. Franklin? Is it possible to resolve this reference problem satisfactorily within the context and setting of the case study? If so, how can this be done? What is your evaluation of the manner in which Miss Massena has handled the entire situation thus far?

23 Home Purchase
of an Encyclopedia

Roger Billings is a professional assistant in the reference department of the Q_____ Public Library, which is generally considered one of the finest large public libraries in the country. Mr. Billings came to his present post immediately after graduation from library school two years ago. He chose to work at Q_____ both because it had an excellent reputation as a training-ground for potential administrators, and because he, himself, had been brought up in the east, and wanted to have the experience of living in another part of the country while he was still young and unmarried. He has enjoyed working there, and his superiors have been equally pleased with the quality of his work in the library. Indeed, he has been mentioned by Miss Woodbridge, the Supervisor of Reference Services, as a candidate for the position of First Assistant in the Reference Department which is expected to become vacant in a few months.

Members of the professional staff of the library are encouraged to participate in community affairs, and membership in local groups and organizations is viewed with favor. Accordingly, Mr. Billings, about a year ago, accepted an invitation to join a local service club for men. This group, whose membership is made up largely of younger men in their late twenties and early thirties, carries on a variety of public service projects in the community, including, during recent years, several activities beneficial to the library. Although many of the men in the group are not people whom Billings might have chosen for friends, he has not found the experience of membership in the organization unpleasant, and, indeed, has rather enjoyed most of the group's activities.

One evening, after a meeting of the service club, Mr. Billings fell into conversation with John Asbury, one of the club's officers:

MR. ASBURY: "Roger, you work down at the library, don't you?"

MR. BILLINGS: "That's right, John. In the reference department."

MR. ASBURY: "I thought you did. You know, I was going to call you up last night. As a matter of fact, I wanted to, but my wife thought I shouldn't bother you."

MR. BILLINGS: "Well, I'm sorry you didn't call. I was at home, as a matter of fact."

MR. ASBURY: "I told Helen that we should have called you. Well, actually there's no harm done, but what I wanted to find out from you was what you thought of the *X_____ Encyclopedia.* Have you heard of it?"

MR. BILLINGS: "Sure, I have. It's a standard reference work. Most libraries have it, including ours."

MR. ASBURY: "I'm glad to hear that. You people recommend it, then?"

MR. BILLINGS: "John, I'm not sure that I'm following you. How do you mean, 'recommend it'?"

MR. ASBURY: "I mean, is it the one that you recommend for people to buy?"

MR. BILLINGS: "Well, that depends. Why? Did you buy it?"

MR. ASBURY: "Gosh, there's nothing wrong with it, is there?"

MR. BILLINGS: "No, there's nothing *wrong* with it, that's not the point. The point is that if you're selecting an encyclopedia, there are a number of factors you would want to consider. You see, there are several excellent encyclopedias, each one of which is slightly different from the others. When you choose one, you ought to choose it from the point of view of the specific features that will be most important, depending on who the people are that are going to use it. If you're considering buying an encyclopedia for yourself, what I'd suggest you do is to come down to the library, look over the encyclopedias that we have, and let us show you some reviews of them written by experts in the field. That way, you can select the one that's right for your particular needs."

MR. ASBURY: "Well, actually, Roger, it's not for me anyway. Helen has been after me to get one, for the kids. Johnny's going into the third grade in September, you know, and my little girl is starting school next year, too. But, to get back to this encyclopedia, what do you really think of it? I'd certainly appreciate your opinion."

MR. BILLINGS: "Do you have just the two children?"

MR. ASBURY: "That's right."

MR. BILLINGS: "Let's see, your little boy would be about eight or nine?"

MR. ASBURY: "Eight."

MR. BILLINGS: "And your little girl?"

MR. ASBURY: "Six in July."

MR. BILLINGS: "So, the encyclopedia would be just for the four of you, the two children, you and your wife?"

MR. ASBURY: "Well, mostly for the kids. To tell you the truth, Roger, I'm ashamed to say it, but I haven't been inside a library since I got out of high school 10, 12 years ago. Actually, that's why I wanted to ask your advice about the encyclopedia. I just don't know anything about them, at all, and I thought that, working in the library, you would. So tell me, what do you think?"

MR. BILLINGS: "John, if you want my honest opinion, I think it's going to be some time before your children will be able to use that particular encyclopedia. If I were you, I'd think about buying something a little less sophisticated for them right now, and hold off on the X_____ until they're older. After all, you wouldn't go out and buy an expensive car today, if you weren't going to be able to drive it until five years from now, would you? You'd wait, so as to buy the latest and most up-to-date model when you were ready to drive it. And, just like a car, an encyclopedia, particularly the one you're considering, is a pretty expensive proposition."

MR. ASBURY: "Let me ask you something. If you were going to buy an encyclopedia for yourself—I mean, you're a librarian and you know about these things—would you buy this one?"

MR. BILLINGS: "To tell you the truth, I wouldn't buy any encyclopedia brand new. I suppose I shouldn't say this, but if I were in your shoes, and wanted an encyclopedia, I'd go to the _____ Book Store, downtown, and buy myself the most recent printing of a good encyclopedia that I could get under a hundred dollars. Then I'd buy the paperback edition of the *World Almanac* every year, and I'd be willing to bet you that for the questions you couldn't answer satisfactorily out of one of those two sources, you could take your whole family to the library in a taxi, have dinner downtown in a good restaurant, and still be money ahead. I just think that new encyclopedias are much too expensive, especially when you realize that only a comparatively small portion of any encyclopedia on the market today is actually up-to-date."

MR. ASBURY: "I don't understand. The one we're talking about is brand new, this year's edition, isn't it?"

Mr. Billings explained briefly to Mr. Asbury the concept of continuous revision as it is currently employed by encyclopedia publishers. In response to a question from Mr. Asbury, Mr. Billings indicated the approximate cost of a new printing of the X_____ *Encyclopedia,* if one were to be purchased by the Q_____ Public Library. Mr. Asbury indicated that he had been quoted a price considerably higher than the figure mentioned by Mr. Billings. The two men continued their conversation:

MR. ASBURY: "Roger, I'm certainly glad I talked with you tonight about this. I'm going to call Jim Solvay when I get home, and tell him to cancel my order. Why, he told us this was a special deal, and the way he explained it, the whole package was a real buy. I see now that there's a lot more to this business than he told us."

MR. BILLINGS: "Let me get this straight. You've signed up for some sort of 'package deal'? Does this involve buying other things besides the encyclopedia?"

MR. ASBURY: "That's the whole point. Solvay told us you couldn't buy it any other way—you have to take the supplements for, I think it's ten years, and, of course, the bookcase and the globe, and—well, there's something else, I can't remember right now, but it's all one price for the whole deal, I do remember that."

MR. BILLINGS: "You mean this salesman told you that you couldn't buy the encyclopedia alone? That you *had* to buy all these other things in order to get the encyclopedia?"

MR. ASBURY: "Right! That's what he said. And now you tell me that isn't so?"

MR. BILLINGS: "It certainly isn't. As a matter of fact, I think that, if I'm not mistaken, the Federal Trade Commission has condemned these package deals with encyclopedias, where the salesman tells you that you can't buy the encyclopedia all by itself."

MR. ASBURY: "I just can't get over this. I grew up with Jim Solvay's younger brother, Ted. I've known Jim all my life. Believe me, I'm going home and call him, and give him a piece of my mind."

MR. BILLINGS: "John, I'm afraid that won't do you much good."

MR. ASBURY: "Well, I'm certainly going to cancel that order."

MR. BILLINGS: "The trouble is, I don't think you'll be able to cancel it. Did you or your wife actually sign something?"

MR. ASBURY: "Just the order blank, that's all."

MR. BILLINGS: "My guess would be that what you signed was actually an 'agreement to purchase,' and if you did, this is legally binding and probably unbreakable. I would be very surprised if Solvay will let you cancel your order."

MR. ASBURY: "What do you mean, not let me cancel? I never heard of anything like that, Roger, and I've been in the hardware business for over ten years. You can always cancel an order, if the item hasn't already been delivered, or if you're not completely satisfied with the product."

MR. BILLINGS: "John, all I can tell you is that, in all likelihood, what you have signed, no matter what it looked like, is an 'agreement to purchase'—a contract, if you will—and I can assure you it's probably ironclad. I've known people who've tried to break these contracts, but I'm afraid any lawyer would tell you that they can't be broken.'"

MR. ASBURY: "Well, I certainly don't intend to get stuck with this encyclopedia. Not after what you've told me. Why, the way Solvay presented this thing to us, we weren't committing ourselves to anything. I can tell you that I have no intention of letting him get away with this kind of shady practice. If you ask me, it smacks of fraud. I don't think that a man who engages in this kind of salesmanship ought to be doing business in this city. Why, Jim Solvay's a member of the Chamber of Commerce, just like I am, and we've got some kind of standards of ethical business practice that our members are supposed to live up to."

MR. BILLINGS: "I think that if Solvay is unwilling to tear up your purchase contract, and my guess is that he won't be willing to, then your only hope is to threaten to expose him for misrepresentation and fraudulent sales practice. You could certainly threaten to go to the Better Business Bureau, or to the attorney general, if necessary. Better still, the local newspaper. Do you think they'd be interested in this?"

MR. ASBURY: "I'm sure they would. I know the people down there pretty well. For one thing, they carry a good deal of our advertising. I think I could make things very unpleasant for Jim Solvay, and the way I feel right now, he'd better come up with some pretty good answers when I talk with him tonight, if he wants to keep on doing business in this town."

MR. BILLINGS: "Let me just give you one other piece of advice on this. Instead of talking to this chap on the telephone tonight, why not ask him to come over to your house instead? Without telling him what you want to see him about. Then, when he comes, make sure your wife's there, and get a third person if possible—perhaps a neighbor. You could always say that the neighbor had heard you were buying the encyclopedia, and thought he might be interested in one too. Then I'd confront Solvay with some of these things, in front of witnesses."

MR. ASBURY: "I think you're right. That *would* be a better way to handle it. Incidentally, that Federal Trade thing you mentioned. Where could I get hold of that?"

MR. BILLINGS: "I'm sure we have it at the library. If you like, I could look it up for you tomorrow, and have a copy made. Would you like me to do that?"

MR. ASBURY: "Yes, I'd be very grateful if you would."

MR. BILLINGS: "All right. I'll do it first thing tomorrow."

MR. ASBURY: "Should I come down to the library and pick it up?"

MR. BILLINGS: "You don't need to. Why don't I just drop it in the mail to you. I'll have a photocopy made."

The two men continued their conversation for a few minutes, although nothing further was said about the matter of the encyclopedia. They parted in a friendly fashion, each returning to his own home.

On the following day, Mr. Billings reported to the library shortly after noon, since he wished to find the material that he had promised to look up for Mr. Asbury, and to have a photocopy made, before going on duty at the reference desk. He located it in a back issue of *Subscription Books Bulletin* (October, 1940), had a photocopy made, and put it into the mail.

Two days passed uneventfully, but on the third day following his conversation with Mr. Asbury, Mr. Billings was notified, when he arrived at the library in the morning, that he was to report to Miss Woodbridge's office before going to the reference room. When he arrived at her office, Miss Woodbridge greeted him in a cordial fashion, and invited him to sit down. Then she said: "Mr. Billings, I asked to see you this morning because I have a rather serious problem on my hands. Before I get to that, however, I want to ask you if you are aware of the contents of this manual?"

Miss Woodbridge produced a copy of a looseleaf notebook which Mr. Billings recognized immediately as the official manual of policies and procedures for the Reference Department of the Q_____ Public Library. He indicated, in response to Miss Woodbridge's question, that he was indeed familiar with its contents.

MISS WOODBRIDGE: "Then, you are aware of our policy for handling requests for advice from library patrons concerning the purchase of reference books for the home?"

MR. BILLINGS: "Yes, I think so. I know that members of the staff are not supposed to make personal judgments in recommending for or against the purchase of specific reference works, but that we are supposed to urge people to examine our copies of reference books, to show them where reviews can be found, and that sort of thing."

MISS WOODBRIDGE: "That's approximately correct. Actually, our policy in this instance is modelled on the policy adopted by the Enoch Pratt Free Library, where these inquiries are handled in about this way. I might add, as you probably are aware, that many public libraries follow a similar policy. But tell me, do you approve of such a policy, yourself?"

MR. BILLINGS: "Well, to tell you the truth, I've never really thought about it before. I'm not sure if I do or not. But, I can tell you one thing. You can be quite sure that I wouldn't consciously violate it, or any other policy of the library, for that matter."

MISS WOODBRIDGE: "I'm very glad to hear that. Now, let me explain why I wanted to see you this morning. Do you know Mr. Solvay, the local representative of the *X*_____ *Encyclopedia?*"

MR. BILLINGS: "No, I've never met the man."

MISS WOODBRIDGE: "Well, I do know Mr. Solvay. In fact, I've known him for a good many years. I might say too that, in spite of the fact that we do not do business with him directly, since, of course, the *X*_____ *Encyclopedia* maintains a separate sales force for institutional sales, he *has* been helpful to the library on occasion over the years. Some years ago, for example, he contributed very generously to help defray the costs of the large exhibit cases that we have in the main lobby. I think it is fair to say that he has been a good friend, both to the library and to the reference department. In any event, late yesterday afternoon, Mr. Solvay telephoned me. I won't go into our conversation in detail, except to say that it was lengthy and very painful. The essence of it seemed to be that Mr. Solvay is accusing you of interfering in a sales relationship between himself and a family by the name of Asbury. Do you know anything about this?"

Mr. Billings responded by recounting in some detail his conversation with John Asbury. He explained how he had come to know Asbury and to talk with him about the encyclopedia; that he had advised him against purchasing the *X*_____ *Encyclopedia* because he felt it was too sophisticated to be useful to Asbury's family at present; and that he had suggested various means by which Asbury might arrange to be released from any contractual obligation to the encyclopedia publisher. He also indicated that he had brought the regulations of the Federal Trade Commission concerning improper practices in encyclopedia sales to Mr. Asbury's attention. He concluded by pointing out that he felt this was a personal, rather than a library matter, that he had advised Mr. Asbury as a friend rather than in any professional capacity, and that all of these things had been done wholly on his own time, rather than during working hours.

Miss Woodbridge listened with great interest to Mr. Billings' recitation of the facts, after which, she said: "Mr. Billings, I appreciate your candor in explaining your involvement in this matter so fully to me. Let me begin by saying that you must know by now my own high opinion of you, in terms of the quality of your work during the two years you have served in this department. You are a fine person, and a valued member of the staff. You may be sure that the administration of the library has been made aware of these things, and that your future prospects here at Q_____ are very bright indeed. I hope shortly to be able to recommend you for the position of First Assistant in the department. Quite beyond that, I shall, in a few years, reach the mandatory retirement age, and, at that time, you would, unquestionably, be a strong candidate to succeed me as head of the department. I must say that the prospect of this pleases me very much, because I do not know a better person to carry on our tradition of service. I am telling you these things because I do want you to understand that you could not have made a more favorable impression than you have during the two years that you have been here, and because I want you to know that you are extremely well thought of. Let me also add that I think you are quite correct in saying that, unless Mr. Asbury's children are prodigies, the X_____ Encyclopedia would be a poor choice for them at this time.

"Now, I think you know me well enough to know that I have never been hesitant in drawing your attention to any errors or limitations on your part that I felt needed to be corrected. I try not to be a carping old woman, and not to criticize the members of my staff unless I feel that an error is fairly serious. On the other hand, as your supervisor, I feel I have a responsibility to you to share with you the things I have learned over the years, and to help you to grow both as a person and as a librarian.

"I don't want to make a long speech about this, but we are dealing here with a problem that I think is both complicated and serious, so please hear me out, and then I'll give you the opportunity to react to what I am going to say. I must tell you that I feel that, in this instance, you have been guilty of several serious errors in judgment that may well have very unpleasant consequences both for me and for the library. You have violated, although I am sure quite unwittingly, not one, but two of the policies that govern the conduct of members of the professional staff of this department. In the first place, you *have* given advice regarding the purchase of a specific reference work, even though, as a matter of library policy, members of the staff are prohibited from giving such advice to the public. The reasons for the existence of this policy should be clear to you, and if they are not, I am sure that they will be before this business with Mr. Solvay is finished. We are a publicly supported institution. As such, we cannot put ourselves in the position of recommending the products of any specific publisher or salesman. Indeed, it is precisely because we are librarians, and because our judgment *can* carry so much weight with a layman, that we *must* not advise for or against the purchase of any specific reference book. Moreover, Mr. Solvay, like the other local representatives of the major encyclopedias, is a businessman and a taxpayer in this community, and we have no right to do anything that might jeopardize his business relationships with his customers.

"There is a practical problem here, too, and it lies in the fact that the home sale of encyclopedias is an extremely competitive business.

Encyclopedia salesmen are very sensitive to anything a librarian might say that could be considered detrimental to the reputation of the product they sell. Several years ago, I made the mistake of pointing out, in a book review, a very minor limitation of one of the well-known encyclopedias. I can tell you that the local salesman for that encyclopedia badgered the life out of me for months afterwards to make a retraction. I learned my lesson from that experience, which, I assure you, was not pleasant.

"The other thing you have done, and this seems to me equally serious, is to take advantage of your position here to give what can only be interpreted as 'legal' advice to your friend, Mr. Asbury. Now I am sure you know that, as a matter of stated policy, we do not, here in the reference department, answer medical or legal questions. This is not only inappropriate, but under certain circumstances unethical.

"Let me add just one more thing. In my opinion, the fact that you were not on duty in the library when you became involved in this situation with Mr. Asbury is completely irrelevant to the issue. As a librarian, you are a professional librarian 24 hours a day, seven days a week. A physician does not stop being a physician at five o'clock in the afternoon when he leaves his office. What I am trying to say to you is that when someone asks your advice about a problem involving an expression of your professional judgment, then you are acting in your capacity as a professional librarian, rather than as a private individual. To me, this means you are bound to observe the policies of this library both inside and outside of its walls, as long as you are a member of its professional staff. Now, I should like to know your reactions to this."

Mr. Billings was silent for a moment or two, and then responded: "Well, there are several things I'd like to say, just to express my own point of view about it. I certainly appreciate your comments on my work here. I can only say, Miss Woodbridge, that I have valued our relationship very much, indeed, and that, quite sincerely, I have only the greatest respect and admiration for you. I know I have learned a great deal from you, and I consider myself extremely fortunate to have had my first working experience here. I am sorry if I have inadvertently created an awkward or difficult situation for you with Mr. Solvay, and I certainly would not, for the world, have done anything that might embarrass you or the library in any way. If I have made a mistake here, I want you to know I am ready to take full responsibility for it.

"Miss Woodbridge, as long as I have known you, I have always found you a fair-minded person. You've invited me to reply to your analysis of this situation, and while I don't for a moment mean to seem disrespectful or to discount your experience, I must say that it seems to me you're overlooking some very important aspects of this. In the first place, John Asbury is my friend. He also happens to be in the hardware business. Now, I am sure that if I needed some advice about hardware, I could depend on John to give me the best and most honest advice he was capable of, precisely because he *is* my friend. It seems to me this is an obligation of friendship, and if such a situation arose, and I were to turn to John for advice, I would be shocked and bitterly disappointed if he were to refuse to give it. I just cannot believe you mean to suggest that simply because I happen to be a librarian, and a librarian is a professional person, I am not at liberty to give advice to a friend on a subject I know something about.

"If you'll allow me just another minute or two, I'd like to get something else off my chest. This Solvay person may be a local businessman, and a benefactor of the library, and all that, but he also happens, in my opinion, to be a pretty shabby specimen as far as the ethics of a business relationship are concerned. He misrepresented himself and his product to the Asburys, and if you ask me, if anybody is entitled to our protection, it's the Asburys, and not Mr. Solvay. I'm sure I don't need to point out to you that the Asburys are *also* taxpayers in this community. Don't we have some obligations to them?

"You made the analogy a few minutes ago between a professional librarian and a physician. I quite agree that if we, as librarians, want to be considered professional people in the community, then we have got to act like professional people. Now, this is my whole quarrel with the library's policy of not making recommendations when people ask our advice about reference books. I would be inclined to say that we are obligated to give the people of this community the benefit of our best professional judgment whenever we are asked for it. I think that when we fail to do this, as in the case of this particular policy, we are actually guilty of *evading* our professional responsibilities. Suppose for a moment that you were to go to a physician with some complaint or other, and he were to say, 'Miss Woodbridge, here is a list of 15 different drugs and treatments that are currently available to treat your illness. Now, here is a sheaf of laboratory reports and results of experiments describing and evaluating each of these treatments. I suggest you read these over, and then, you must decide which drug or treatment you think would be best for you to take. I cannot tell you which one to take, because it would be unethical for me to be in the position of promoting the use of any particular drug over the products of other drug companies. Of course, I know that some of these drugs and treatments would be better for you than others, because of your specific symptoms, but you'll have to decide for yourself, without any further help from me, which one to take.' It seems ridiculous, doesn't it? Yet, doesn't the analogy hold with respect to our giving people the benefit of our best professional judgment when they are considering investing several hundred dollars in an encyclopedia, and don't know which one to choose? Now, do you see why I have some reservations about our policy here?"

How do you evaluate the positions taken by Miss Woodbridge and Mr. Billings respectively? Do you consider Mr. Billings' advice to the Asburys against the purchase of *any* new encyclopedia sound? If you were Miss Woodbridge, how would you respond to the questions Mr. Billings has raised? What further action would you take, if you were Miss Woodbridge, with respect to Mr. Solvay? If Mr. Billings is called upon, as a friend, by Mr. Asbury for further advice on this matter, how should he respond? Is Miss Woodbridge correct when she says that most public libraries do not give advice to library patrons concerning the purchase of specific reference books, but limit themselves to making sets available for examination and referring patrons to reviews? Was Miss Woodbridge correct in criticizing Mr. Billings for his apparent violations of library and departmental policy?

24 An Inquiry by a Trustee

Alfred Hanson is the recently appointed director of the F_____ Public Library, which serves a community on the outer suburban fringe of a large metropolitan center in the northeastern United States. F_____ is a residential community, a town of fine homes and comparatively well-to-do suburbanites, and because it is located a considerable distance away from the city, its population has tended to grow rather slowly in comparison with neighboring suburbs that are closer to the city. The present population of F_____ is slightly over 12,000.

In its government and politics, F_____ has always been a conservative community. Its conservatism, especially in fiscal matters, is reflected in the present state of the F_____ Public Library, which in the more than 50 years of its existence, has survived on a budget that would have been inadequate for a library serving a community one-fourth the size of F_____. Its board of trustees, for many years, had no concept of the inadequacies of the library, nor any understanding or awareness of modern library practice. The library was staffed by two local women of advanced years, one of whom, Miss Avon, had served as librarian since 1924. Neither Miss Avon, nor her aged assistant, Miss Peekskill, had had any training for librarianship, nor, indeed, had either of them had any formal education beyond high school.

Two years before the time of the events described in this case study, the F_____ League of Women Voters undertook a "survey" of the library. In the beginning, neither the librarians, nor the board of trustees, had taken this very seriously, but as the study developed, it soon became apparent that the organization had found a "cause" and intended to make the climate an uncomfortable one for the administration of the library. Outside assistance was sought from the state library extension agency, which sent a field worker into F_____ to assist the League in its investigations. The results of the survey were even more shocking than anyone in the community might have expected. The report, widely publicized in the local press, termed the library "the shame of the community," and one of the poorest in the state. It was criticized for its unattractive building, and for a book collection that was described in the report, and subsequently in the local press, as "so inadequate and antiquated as to represent a positive danger to this community, and particularly to its young people."

The chairman of the library survey committee, and the driving force behind the whole movement towards library improvement, was a comparative newcomer to the community, Mrs. Elizabeth Norman. Mrs. Norman was a forceful and dynamic woman, the wife of a well-to-do architect. She was determined not to be ignored, and she took full advantage of every opportunity to point out publicly the limitations of the F_____ Public Library. She insisted in presenting her committee's report to the library trustees in person, and when the board failed to respond to her request to meet with them, she organized a "mother's march for better libraries." This group of women campaigned successfully to bring about the election of Mrs. Norman to a vacant position on the board of trustees.

After a few months, a second member of the library board resigned, ostensibly because of ill-health, but actually, as he confided to a friend, because he was "sick and tired of listening to that Norman woman make speeches at every board meeting." A close supporter of Mrs. Norman was appointed to fill the vacancy, and the two ladies next set to work to convince Miss Avon of the wisdom of early retirement. It took almost a year to wear Miss Avon down to the point where, seeing the folly of any further resistance, she reluctantly affixed her signature to a carefully-worded letter of resignation that Mrs. Norman had thoughtfully prepared months earlier. In due course, despite the opposition of a large segment of the community who would have preferred a local person, Mr. Hanson was brought to F_____ from a nontitular position in a nearby public library, to succeed Miss Avon. Mrs. Norman was jubilant, and did not hesitate to let it be known, both to Mr. Hanson and to the community, that she and Mrs. Carlisle, her single supporter on the library board, were responsible for the appointment.

Mr. Hanson came to F_____ with a clear awareness of the limitations of the library, but in the sincere belief that there existed, both in the community and in the library board, what he called "a climate receptive to change." During his first few weeks on the job, he worked assiduously in developing plans to provide the kind of book collection, staff and facilities needed to support modern library service. Mrs. Norman was a tower of strength, lending her support in convincing other members of the board of the necessity for implementing his plans, helping to recruit clerical and secretarial staff, and arranging for Mr. Hanson to meet with a variety of community groups and civic organizations. Three months after his arrival, even Mr. Hanson, who was young and impatient for change, marvelled at how much had been accomplished in putting the F＿＿＿ Public Library back on its feet.

One morning, Mr. Hanson received a telephone call at his office from Mrs. Norman. The conversation centered initially around several recommendations that Mr. Hanson intended to present at the next meeting of the board of trustees. Without hesitation, Mrs. Norman promised to support all of his proposals at the forthcoming meeting, adding that she was most impressed by his achievement thus far at F＿＿＿, and predicting a glowing future both for the library and for Alfred Hanson. She then said that she had one other matter to discuss with him, and the conversation continued as follows:

MRS. NORMAN: "Mr. Hanson, I wonder if you could do me a personal favor?"

MR. HANSON: "Why certainly. What would that be?"

MRS. NORMAN: "Tell me first, do you have anything in the library that is later than the *World Almanac*?"

MR. HANSON: "Mrs. Norman, I'm not quite sure I follow you. How do you mean, later than the *World Almanac*?"

MRS. NORMAN: "Let me explain. I'm trying to find the names of the American ambassadors in three countries: Peru, Finland and Turkey. I have this year's *World Almanac* at home, which lists the names of ambassadors, but I'm sure it's out of date. It's dated December first of last year, and here it is almost September. Now, do you have anything more recent?"

MR. HANSON: "I'm not really sure what we might have that would give a more up-to-date list. Peru, Turkey and Finland, is that it?"

MRS. NORMAN: "That's right. I wouldn't be troubling you with this, Mr. Hanson, because I know how busy you are, but I've exhausted my own resources here at home, and it's quite important to me to have this information this afternoon. I just daren't rely on this list in the *World Almanac* as being up-to-date enough for my purposes. I know what an ingenious person you are, and you've been so helpful in finding things for me in the past."

MR. HANSON: "I'll tell you what. Let me have a look around and call you back. It's quarter to eleven now. How long will you be at home?"

MRS. NORMAN: "Until two o'clock."

MR. HANSON: "Well, I'll see what I can dig up here, and call you back before two."

At the conclusion of the conversation, Mr. Hanson thought for a few moments about the information that Mrs. Norman needed. Since he was not completely familiar with the reference sources in the library, he walked out to the reference room, and examined the yearbooks, almanacs, and other annuals on the shelves. Beyond the current issue of the *World Almanac,* and a two-year-old copy of the *Statesman's Yearbook,* there was nothing up-to-date or even remotely relevant to the problem. He reflected that if the problem had arisen in the large public library where he had formerly been employed, he would have searched the *New York Times Index* and *Facts on File* for the current year, in order to bring the information in the *World Almanac* up-to-date. Unfortunately, the F_____ Public Library did not subscribe to either of these services, and, indeed, did not even maintain any back files of newspapers, except for the local weekly, which was unlikely to contain information of the kind he was seeking. He considered the possibility of telephoning the Z_____ Public Library, the nearest large public library to F_____, but decided against it because it involved a long distance call, and he felt the question was too complex to be handled by telephone.

Is it possible for Mr. Hanson to locate the information that Mrs. Norman has asked for within the time available? Given the resources that are known to be available, or might reasonably be expected to be available at the F_____ Public Library, what steps would you recommend he take in order to resolve the problem and supply the desired facts?

Do you feel, in general, that a public library serving a community of 12,000 people like F_____ should be prepared to handle the kind of informational request represented by Mrs. Norman's question? Would the resources that would be required to provide a prompt, accurate answer to her question be beyond the means of a public library this size?

25 Instruction in Use
of the Library

T_____ Community College is a small, two-year institution, founded as an experiment in higher education. It is the first tax-supported college of its kind in the state in which it is located. There are, however, within the state, a number of fine, private four-year colleges, many of which are church–affiliated, as well as an excellent state-supported, land grant university, with strong graduate and professional programs.

Several years ago, the legislature appointed a citizen's fact-finding committee to investigate opportunities for higher education in the state. The committee conducted studies with the assistance of a firm of educational consultants, held public hearings, and made a two-week trip to California to investigate public higher education there. In its report to the legislature, the committee noted that many talented young people were unable to finance the costs of four years of college away from home, and accordingly were deprived of the opportunity for education beyond high school. Although tuition at the state university was nominal, residence fees were sufficiently high to deter many otherwise qualified students from attending.

The committee considered in its report the phenomenon of the "late-blooming" adolescent, the young person possessed of considerable intellectual potential who fails to mature academically in secondary school, and whose high school grades do not reflect his true ability. The report also noted a significant shortage within the state of trained technicians in a variety of fields, and the lack of educational facilities offering training in such areas as aviation technology, practical nursing, dental hygiene, and electronics.

The committee accordingly recommended the immediate establishment of a system of publicly supported community colleges throughout the state, in order to provide a fuller range of educational opportunities. It was suggested that ten such institutions, offering the first two years of the liberal arts curriculum as well as one or more technical programs of a terminal nature, would be needed. In the preface to the report, the committee acknowledged that it had drawn heavily upon the California plan for public junior colleges in formulating its recommendations.

After numerous delays, and in the face of considerable opposition from conservative elements, the state legislature at length appropriated funds to establish a single, state-supported, community college at T_____ for an experimental four-year period. Upon the success of this institution depended any future appropriations for additional community colleges.

The college was officially opened one year later in temporary quarters in a renovated building which had formerly housed the offices of another state agency. In lieu of a formal catalog, the college prepared a brief statement of aims and programs of study, which is included as an appendix to this case. The college is governed by an unpaid board of trustees, appointed by the governor of the state, and numbering among its members three professional educators as well as an equal number of well-known political figures, including a former state senator. After considering several candidates for the post of executive director of the college, the board of trustees appointed Dr. Edward Atwater.

Dr. Atwater was, in some respects, an excellent choice as the first director of T_____ Community College. He was 37 years old at the time of his appointment, and held the degree of Doctor of Education, with a specialization in educational administration, from the state university. After a brief period as instructor in history at a small college, Atwater had returned to his alma mater as assistant to the dean of men. Two years later, while he was still completing his doctoral work in education, he was given responsibility for a university fund drive, and scored a spectacular success by raising nearly three million dollars in alumni gifts and pledges. In his next post, as president of J_____ Junior College, a privately supported institution, he nearly doubled faculty salaries within four years, obtained federal loans for the construction of three dormitories, and secured a foundation grant for a new science building. He guided the college into an extensive adult education program, and J_____, which had heretofore been virtually unknown, suddenly was pleasantly surprised to find itself described in a national, mass-circulation magazine as "a vital center of community education." The same magazine article identified Dr. Atwater as "J_____'s dynamic, progressive young president," and brought him to the attention of the T_____ Board of Trustees at the very moment the Board was seeking its first executive director.

Dr. Atwater's decision to come to T_____ was not made lightly. He realized, of course, that the future of the college was uncertain, and that there was an element of risk involved in terms of his own career, should the experiment fail. On the other hand, he was able to demand and get an attractive salary, as well as a pledge of non-interference in the operation of the college on the part of the board of trustees. The chairman of the board, moreover, held out the possibility that Atwater would be in line for the post of chief administrator of community colleges for the entire state, in the event additional colleges were established in the future. This possibility was indeed attractive, and proved decisive in bringing Atwater to T_____. He arrived on the scene ten months before the college was scheduled to open its doors to the first class.

Atwater was determined that the T_____ experiment should be a success, and worked hard to make it one. A 12-hour working day was not unusual for him during this period. Of the many problems that claimed his attention, the recruitment of faculty and staff received a major share of his time and efforts. Discussing this problem with the chairman of his board, George Ambler, one day at lunch shortly after his arrival, Dr. Atwater described it thus:

ATWATER: "You see, George, T_____ is an unusual institution, not like the traditional liberal arts college. Sure, we'll get a few kids with SAT scores of 600 or better, good enough to get them into Ivy League colleges if they wanted to go there, and could afford to. We'll also get our share of kids with scores in the 300's, too low to be considered for any decent college. Frankly, we've got to build up enrollment in these next few years, and we're not going to be in any position to reject these people, even if we wanted to."

AMBLER: "Not only that, Ed, but we have to consider the political situation too. If you don't let these people in, and their parents start to pressure some of the members of the legislature, we're going to be out of business in four years, when the time comes to renew our appropriation."

ATWATER: "Right! And when it comes to the faculty, we've got to think in terms of the kind of student we're going to have. My own thinking is that people trained primarily in education are likely to be more sympathetic with our aims, and function better in our kind of situation."

AMBLER: "Do you mean that we ought to recruit our faculty from secondary schools, rather than the colleges?"

ATWATER: "Exactly. I'd like to see at least half the faculty composed of people who've taught at the secondary school level."

AMBLER: "Why not the whole faculty?"

ATWATER: "George, unfortunately, it's not that simple. For one thing, there's the matter of accreditation. Don't forget, we've got a transfer program in liberal arts as well as our terminal programs. I know that State has already indicated that they're willing to take our graduates as transfer students with junior standing, but students from our liberal arts program have got to be able to get into other colleges too. That means we've got to be accredited, and accredited as soon as possible. Our regional accrediting group would frown on the idea of a faculty without Ph.D.'s. We'll have to get people from the college teaching field. I want to avoid getting teachers who are too heavily committed to research. I have always thought that one of the troubles with most of our colleges is that we've too many people who are primarily oriented towards research and publication, rather than teaching. I want people who are good teachers, and I don't care if they never publish a thing. Also, they've got to be able to teach the kind of student we're going to have at T____. Now, don't get me wrong. Our liberal arts program will be strictly college level, not watered down in any respect. But, on the other hand, it's not going to be Princeton or Harvard either."

AMBLER: "I know that, Ed, and frankly, it seems to me you've got the right idea about faculty. You go ahead and get the kind of people you want, as long as you're sure they'll be acceptable to an accrediting committee."

ATWATER: "George, while we're discussing accreditation, there's one other point I'd like to raise, and that's the matter of our library. I don't know if you're aware of this, or not, but the library will be an important part of the picture in terms of accreditation. I'm especially conscious of this, because while I was at J____, we discovered that our library was below standard. As a matter of fact, we had to develop a crash program there to beef up the library, or we might have run into real trouble. I don't want anything like that to happen here, so I'm proposing a positive approach from the very beginning."

AMBLER: "That's fine, Ed. Now this sort of thing, as far as I'm concerned, is entirely within your province as director of the college. Is there anything you'll need as far as the board is concerned?"

ATWATER: "Well, we'll need to hire a librarian, probably before college opens in the fall. This shouldn't be any problem. Our salary schedule is a notch above what State pays their faculty, and certainly comparable to salaries in the secondary field. Beyond this, we'll want to put some money into books; I should think initially perhaps $15,000 a year, for three years."

AMBLER: "That's a good deal of money, Ed, but you're the best judge of what's needed."

ATWATER: "I hoped you'd say that, George. I'd like to get approval on this at the board meeting next Monday. Then I can get going on this library thing right away. If I can find a librarian, and a dean, within the next month, then I'll feel we're really under way."

Dr. Atwater was not long in finding a man to fill the post of dean of the college. Frank Shelby, assistant professor of government at L_____ College, a highly respected liberal arts college in the area, was appointed to the position shortly after the conversation recorded above took place. Shelby was in his early forties, undistinguished as a scholar, but well-known for his frequent and highly vocal criticisms of the state of higher education both at L_____ and elsewhere. He rather relished his role as an intellectual gadfly, and seemed to take particular delight in holding forth at faculty meetings, where he alternately accused the college of lowering academic standards, what he referred to as "sugar-coating the curriculum," or of inflexibility in failing to modify the program of study to meet 20th Century needs. He had endorsed with equal vigor such seemingly contradictory proposals at L_____ as making Latin a required course of study for freshmen and introducing a program in resort management at the master's degree level. Shelby affected tweeds, a slight British accent, and never made the mistake of seeming to be overly enthusiastic about anything. Some of his colleagues at L_____ considered him mildly eccentric, although he carefully refrained from carrying any eccentricity to the point where it might jeopardize his position there. It may truthfully be said that both the president of L_____ and the chairman of the department of government there breathed a sigh of relief when Shelby announced that he intended to become dean of T_____.

The post of dean at T_____ represented an administrative responsibility of some importance. With a small faculty, Dr. Atwater saw no need for a formal organization along departmental lines, and preferred to centralize administrative responsibility in himself and the dean. The dean was to be primarily responsible for internal administration of the college, and for development of the curriculum. In these terms, the choice of Frank Shelby as dean might seem unusual, although Atwater made it with studied deliberation, and with a full knowledge of the kind of person Shelby was. Both men were ambitious, both for T_____ and for themselves, although each sought to gain his career objectives in a different way. Shelby was genuinely interested in the concept of

T_____ as an educational experiment, and was delighted to have the opportunity to set the instructional tone there, as well as to implement some of his own theories about higher education. Although Atwater made it clear that he intended to interest himself in all matters relating to the curriculum, Shelby felt he would still have a good deal of freedom, and that, should there be a difference of opinion, he could bring Dr. Atwater around to his own point of view. As for Atwater, he felt, as he said to his wife in discussing the appointment, that "Frank has got some very original ideas, and besides, he'll add some tone to the place."

Before Dean Shelby arrived at T_____, Dr. Atwater appointed Lloyd Monson librarian. Monson was a recent graduate of the school of library science at the state university, and, up to the time of his appointment to the post at T_____, had served as a member of the professional staff of the university library.

Mr. Monson was impressed by Dr. Atwater, who seemed to him personable, vigorous and dynamic. During their initial interview, they discussed the library in some detail. Atwater indicated the sums available for the purchase of books during the first two years, and stated that he hoped to have approximately 4,000 volumes on the shelves by the beginning of the college year in September. Mr. Monson said that since he would be unable even to come to T_____ before May 1, this seemed an impossible assignment for the four months that remained before the opening of the college, but that he would be willing to "do his best."

Monson arrived on the scene May 1, as he had promised. He found that reasonably adequate space had been provided in the remodeled building for the library, and that furniture and equipment had already been installed. His initial task was to select, acquire and organize a basic book collection as quickly as possible. Dr. Atwater had provided a full-time clerical assistant, as well as a high school boy who worked after school and on Saturdays. Mr. Monson understood that no additional staff would be provided during the first year, so that he was expected to serve as cataloger and reference librarian in addition to his administrative duties. The circulation desk, according to Dr. Atwater's plans, was to be manned by part-time student assistants once the school opened in the fall.

Mr. Monson set to work immediately and quickly established relationships with a book jobber who would supply the bulk of the library's book needs, as well as with the Library of Congress for the purchase of printed catalog cards. He obtained copies of several standard book selection aids for public and academic libraries, and went through them, checking titles to be ordered. His clerical assistant, using multiple-copy book order forms, typed orders for books and printed catalog cards, added classification numbers and subject headings to the cards as they were received, and filed them in the catalog. The high school boy handled shipments of books, unpacked cartons, lettered call numbers on the volumes, and placed the finished books on the shelves. Library of Congress suggested decimal classification numbers and subject headings were accepted as they appeared on the printed cards, so that cataloging became wholly a clerical process. By August 1, nearly 700 books were on the shelves, and with shipments arriving almost daily, Mr. Monson expected that perhaps twice that number might be available for student use by opening day. He anticipated that book ordering, cataloging and processing would continue throughout the academic year, and that the bulk of his own time, and the time of his two assistants, would be devoted to these activities.

One day, early in August, Mr. Monson had a telephone call from Dr. Atwater's secretary, asking that he meet with Dr. Atwater at 9 a.m. the following morning. When he arrived at Atwater's office, he found the director, as well as Dean Shelby, waiting for him.

DR. ATWATER: "Come in, Lloyd, come in. You know Frank, don't you?"

MR. MONSON: "Yes. We met about a month ago."

DR. ATWATER: "Right! Frank's been on the road most of the last two weeks, trying to round up some faculty for this place."

MR. MONSON: "I hope you've been successful."

DEAN SHELBY: "Not terribly, Mr. Monson, not terribly. Our needs will not be large, at least initially, but to find the *type* of person we want at T_____ is something of a problem."

DR. ATWATER: "Frank's latched on to one person who'll help us a good deal. Name's Culver. Retired last year from the faculty at teachers college. He'll teach the humanities course for us. We've got a first-rate chap from the local high school to do the shop courses for the terminal program. Frank and I will handle social science, at least for the first year, and Frank's wife has let us persuade her to come in on a part-time basis for the French. So, all we need is a scientist, and we've got ourselves a faculty."

MR. MONSON: "Do you have any idea yet how many students there will be in the entering class?"

DR. ATWATER: "I've got my fingers crossed, Lloyd. We're hoping for a hundred, and we'll take all we can get."

DEAN SHELBY: "Within reasonable standards, of course. Although, I'm sorry to say we may have to compromise a bit, at least for the first year. Fortunately, the weaker applicants, by and large, have been for the terminal programs."

MR. MONSON: "How large will the group in the aviation technology program be?"

DR. ATWATER: "Probably about 30."

MR. MONSON: "And the remaining 70 in the liberal arts transfer program?"

DR. ATWATER: "Or in the business program."

MR. MONSON: "Oh, then you *are* planning to offer the program in business?"

DR. ATWATER: "If we can get enough interested students to make it worthwhile. At the moment, it's tentative. Say, look at the time! Frank, you and I have that meeting at 9:30. Lloyd, I'm afraid we're a bit pressed for time this morning, but I thought we ought to get together and see where we stand on the library. Are you going to have some books for us in September? How's everything going?"

MR. MONSON: "Fairly well. Of course, we've all been working pretty hard, I don't mind saying, but I think we'll have a good part of a basic book collection on the shelves by September."

DR. ATWATER: "I'll say you have been working hard. Frank, I want you and Lloyd here to really get to know one another. I have enormous respect for this man. Wait till you see the job he's done in that library. Fantastic!"

DEAN SHELBY: "I'm sure it is, although frankly, Mr. Monson, I must confess that I've never been able to understand why the business of getting books on the library shelves need be so complicated. But, perhaps you and I might discuss that another time. At the moment, Dr. Atwater is anxious to know your thinking on the matter of library orientation for our students."

MR. MONSON: "Well, I'm afraid you've taken me by surprise on that one. Things have been so hectic since I came that I really hadn't thought about it."

DEAN SHELBY: "Yes, of course. Actually, Mr. Monson, I rather think that perhaps it is unnecessary for us to burden you with this sort of problem. I cannot recall our ever having done anything of this sort at L____, although I don't think our students suffered particularly from the lack of it. It seems to me that the business of finding one's way about in the library is a matter of individual responsibility on the part of the student."

DR. ATWATER: "Why, Frank, perhaps I haven't made clear what I had in mind when I suggested this. It seems to me we have a responsibility here to train our students to work independently, and that's where the library comes in. I hesitate to use the word 'research,' but I think, in a sense at least, that that's what I mean. When I give a student a term paper assignment on, let's say, Garrison and the

Abolitionists, I would expect him to dig out background material on his own, beyond what he gets in lectures and from reading the text. This sort of thing, it seems to me, requires some instruction in, at least, elementary research techniques. Now, this is perhaps less relevant in the terminal programs, but it certainly ought to have a place in the curriculum for the transfer student. Lloyd, have you had any experience with this? How do libraries handle it?"

MR. MONSON: "Actually, we didn't do too much of it at State, although we talked about it a good deal. There never seemed to be time. Personally, I think it's terribly important, particularly on the basis of the experience I've had in working with students who'd been given assignments involving the use of the library. Most of them haven't the faintest idea of how to begin to find material."

DEAN SHELBY: "No doubt that may be true. It does seem to me, though, that this is a matter of instructional responsibility, rather than a library problem."

DR. ATWATER: "Well, now, that's just where I don't agree, Frank —or rather, let me say I see the problem from a little different point of view. It seems to me this might be one area where faculty and librarian could operate cooperatively, perhaps even sharing responsibility for instruction. In fact, if I'm not mistaken, there have been experiments along this line, tied in with the kind of general education program we plan for our liberal arts students."

MR. MONSON: "Yes, there have. In fact, there's an experiment— I think, at Wayne University—where people on the library staff participate directly in the teaching program."

DEAN SHELBY: "How extraordinary! Do you know the details of this?"

MR. MONSON: "No, I don't. I could find out, though."

DR. ATWATER: "I wish you would, Lloyd. I'd be interested in knowing whether we might try something of the sort here, on a very modest scale, of course."

DEAN SHELBY: "If I may say so, I'm not at all certain this would be worth any very detailed or time-consuming investigation. Please don't misunderstand me, Mr. Monson, but I would have serious reservations about any librarian becoming involved in instruction. I just don't think it is a librarian's job. I'm also inclined to think that just because something is done as part of a general education program somewhere else doesn't mean that we need to do it here. There is a good deal of faddism attached to this whole general education movement, which I should certainly hope we could avoid."

DR. ATWATER: "Agreed, Frank! Agreed 100 percent! Still and all, correlating the library with the teaching program intrigues me, and I don't think it would do any harm to discuss it further if Lloyd thinks it has merit. But, to come back down to earth for a minute, and to be specific, Lloyd, we asked you to come by this morning because we're trying to plan a three-day orientation session for new students before college opens in the fall. This will give them a chance to get acquainted before they start going to classes. I had thought a tour of the library, and perhaps some elementary instruction in how to use it, might be appropriate as part of the general orientation. After our discussion this morning, however, I'm inclined to think that perhaps we ought to make some basic decisions about how far we want to go in this whole business of library orientation, so that anything you might want to do during the orientation session would be tied in with our ultimate goals. What do you think?"

MR. MONSON: "I think your point about trying to correlate the teaching program with the library represents an area that I'd like very much to explore. And, of course, anything we might want to do during a general orientation session would have to be determined on the basis of whether this is going to be just a one-shot affair, as far as the library is concerned, or whether the library is to be involved at various stages of the whole curriculum. If you and Dean Shelby would be willing to give me a few days to investigate this a bit, and think it through, I think I'd be prepared to make some recommendations to you. I know that both of you are pressed for time this morning, and I don't mean to prolong our discussion unnecessarily, but I do think that I will have to consider these matters in terms of the total obligations of the library during the coming year. We have a great deal to do in the way of just getting organized, and I don't want to spread myself too thin. I don't think I'd want to recommend anything too ambitious the first year. Perhaps in another year, when things get settled . . ."

DR. ATWATER: "Right, of course. But don't overlook the fact that in another year the basic curriculum and instructional plan of this school is going to be set, and it's going to be hard to change it. If we're going to do any experimenting, this is the year to do it. Now, Lloyd, Frank and I really have run out of time, and we're going to have to ask you to excuse us. What I'd like you to do, if you will, is to think this through during the coming week, find out as much as you can about what other schools are doing, and see if you can come up with some recommendations on instruction in the use of the library that we three can toss around. As far as I'm concerned, this is primarily a matter of your responsibility as our librarian, and our job is to receive your recommendations, and then decide whether or not we want to accept them. You have a fair idea of how Frank and I feel about this question, I'm sure, from our discussion this morning. Now, of course, curriculum planning is Frank's baby, but I'm going to stick my nose in from time to time and Frank has agreed to tolerate this, at least for the moment. I wonder if you would be willing to let us have your thoughts on this, in the form of a memo by, let's say, a week from today? I hate to press you, because I know you have many other things to do, but we've just got to wrap up a program for the orientation session as soon as we can, and if you want to be part of it, we've got to know. As soon as we have your recommendations, we'll schedule another session like this one, and thrash them out."

Mr. Monson agreed to study the matter, prepare a memorandum containing a statement of recommended principles for a program of instruction in the use of the library for T____ College, and have this in the hands of Dr. Atwater and Dean Shelby within a week's time.

The solution of this problem consists of the preparation of a memorandum which embodies principles for a program of instruction in the use of the library for T____ College. Among factors that will need to be considered are the nature of the college and its student body, the curriculum, and the respective points of view of Dr. Atwater and Dean Shelby towards the role of the library in the instructional process.

■ APPENDIX

THE PROGRAM OF STUDY AT T____
COMMUNITY COLLEGE

A STATEMENT OF PURPOSE

T____ Community College is a two-year coeducational public college for commuting students. It aims to offer high quality, low cost education for qualified high school graduates who wish to attend two years of college within commuting distance of home. It provides:

1. Two years of liberal arts transfer education for students who plan to attend the state university, or other four-year institutions, for the last two years of college.

2. Occupational programs, carefully chosen to meet regional needs for trained personnel in business and industry, for students who wish to go to work after two years of college.

3. Guidance services for the student who wants or needs advice in selecting his college program or in determining his occupational goals.

THE PROGRAMS OF STUDY

LIBERAL ARTS PROGRAM (leads to the degree of Associate in Arts—for students who intend to complete the last two years of college elsewhere)

Freshman Year

First semester		Second semester	
English	3 credits	English	3 credits
Mathematics	3 credits	Mathematics	3 credits
Foreign language	3 credits	Foreign language	3 credits
Social Science	3 credits	Social Science	3 credits
Biology	3 credits	Biology	3 credits
Physical education	1 credit	Physical education	1 credit

Sophomore Year

First semester		Second semester	
English literature	3 credits	American literature	3 credits
Physics or Chemistry	4 credits	Physics or Chemistry	4 credits
Foreign language	3 credits	Foreign language	3 credits
Social Science	3 credits	Social Science	3 credits
Fundamentals of art	3 credits	Introduction to music	3 credits

AVIATION TECHNOLOGY PROGRAM (leads to the degree of Associate in Science, and prepares students to work in the aviation industry immediately following their graduation)

Freshman Year

First semester		Second semester	
English	3 credits	English	3 credits
Social Science	3 credits	Social Science	3 credits
Algebra	3 credits	Trigonometry	3 credits
Engineering drawing	2 credits	Engineering drawing	2 credits
Physics	3 credits	Physics	3 credits
DC electricity	4 credits	AC electricity	4 credits
Aerodynamics I	3 credits	Aerodynamics II	3 credits

Sophomore Year

First semester		Second semester	
Humanities	3 credits	Humanities	3 credits
Social Science	3 credits	Social Science	3 credits
Differential equations	3 credits	Differential equations	3 credits
Aircraft stability	4 credits	Structures	4 credits
Propulsion	4 credits	Propulsion	4 credits
Strength of materials	4 credits	Design laboratory	4 credits

BUSINESS PROGRAM (leads to the degree of Associate in Science, and prepares students for positions in business and industry immediately following their graduation)

Freshman Year

First semester			Second semester		
English	3	credits	English	3	credits
Business mathematics	3	credits	Business mathematics	3	credits
Shorthand	3	credits	Shorthand	3	credits
Typewriting	3	credits	Typewriting	3	credits
Social Science	3	credits	Social Science	3	credits
Filing	2	credits	Office machines	2	credits

Sophomore Year

First semester			Second semester		
English	3	credits	Business communications	3	credits
Accounting	3	credits	Accounting	3	credits
Shorthand	3	credits	Shorthand	3	credits
Typewriting	3	credits	Typewriting	3	credits
Business law	2	credits	Business law	2	credits
Human relations	3	credits	Human relations	3	credits

NOTE: The Business program will be offered only if a sufficient number of students indicate interest in it.

26 The Language Tree

The Lanett Memorial Free Public Library is considered one of the finest small libraries in the middle-Atlantic state in which it is located. A budget of $91,000 for the current year provides financial support in excess of five dollars per capita. The library is adequately housed in a municipal building constructed three years ago, which includes all of the facilities needed for modern, efficient service. Among its staff of 11, four hold professional positions for which they have qualified either through professional training or by long experience. The library is noted for its imaginative programs for children, designed to stimulate reading, and for its adult book collection, which reflects the highest standards of good taste, quality and literary judgment.

The community which the Lanett Memorial Free Public Library serves is almost wholly residential in character, and has been especially attractive to executives and professional people, most of whom travel daily to their places of employment in a large city some 35 miles away. Those who live in the region in which the town is located generally refer to it as the "gold coast," an appellation that seems not wholly unwarranted when one considers the fact that the average family income of its residents is nearly $12,000 a year.

The reference collection reflects high standards of quality and careful book selection. The reference shelves, located adjacent to the card catalog and the adult reading room, hold approximately 300 titles, including recent printings of all the major adult and children's encyclopedias, current yearbooks, almanacs and statistical compilations, and a wealth of biographical dictionaries and sourcebooks in various subject fields. The library subscribes to *Facts on File*, the *New York Times Index*, the complete *Moody's Investor's Service*, the *Cumulative Book Index*, *Book Review Digest*, the *Reader's Guide to Periodical*

Literature, Biography Index, and *Current Biography.* Annuals and new editions are purchased as promptly as they appear, and the reference shelves are carefully pruned of deadwood so as to continually constitute an alive, up-to-date, working collection.

A reference desk, located centrally near the card catalog and the reference shelves, is manned by a professional staff member every afternoon and evening. During the mornings, except for Saturdays, comparatively few people come into the library, so that members of the professional staff often take a turn at the circulation desk for an hour or two, since it is not considered necessary to cover the reference desk at such times. Accordingly, Mrs. Eleanor Berwyn, reference librarian, was working at the circulation desk just before noon one day when an attractive, middle-aged woman came up to her.

MRS. BERWYN: "Good morning. Can I do something to help you?"

WOMAN: "Good morning. I'm looking for a copy of the language tree. Do you know if you have one?"

MRS. BERWYN: "The language tree? Is that a new book? I'm afraid that I'm not familiar with it."

WOMAN: "Oh, I'm sorry. It's not a book, that's not what I meant. Haven't you ever seen a language tree?"

MRS. BERWYN: "No, I don't believe that I have. Is it something to do with gardening?"

WOMAN: "Good heavens, no! I guess I'm just not making it very clear. It's a picture, I'm sure you must have seen it."

MRS. BERWYN: "Do you mean a painting?"

WOMAN: "It's not a painting, it's a drawing. It shows how all the languages are related to one another—French, Spanish, German, Russian, all the European languages. They're all shown as branches of a tree, and the trunk of the tree is some Indian language that they all come from."

MRS. BERWYN: "How stupid of me! Now I understand. I have seen a drawing like that, although for the life of me, I can't remember where."

WOMAN: "Do you know if I could find it in the library?"

MRS. BERWYN: "No, offhand I don't."

WOMAN: "Is there any kind of index, or anything, that I could look at?"

MRS. BERWYN: "Well, the only *index* to the holdings of the library is the card catalog, but that wouldn't help very much in this case. I think the best thing to do would be to go through the books in the 400's, that's the classification number for languages, and see if you could find it reproduced in one of those."

WOMAN: "I'll do that. Where are those books kept?"

MRS. BERWYN: "There are a few in the adult reading room right behind you. Those are the newer books. The rest are kept in the stacks. The entrance is over there on your left. It shouldn't take you too long to go through them, actually, because there can't be more than 100 or 150 books in all in that classification. And some of those are dictionaries, which you could probably skip. I'd go with you and help, except that I'm alone here at the desk this morning."

WOMAN: "Oh, that's all right. I understand. I'll go and look through them. I have plenty of time. Thank you."

The woman left the desk, and went into the adult reading room. Mrs. Berwyn watched her long enough to make certain that she had located the non-fiction section of the collection, and then returned to her work at the circulation desk. About a half hour later, the same woman appeared again in front of the desk, carrying two books which she handed to Mrs. Berwyn, along with her library card, for charging. Mrs. Berwyn noticed that both of the books were novels.

MRS. BERWYN: "Didn't you have any luck? Were you able to find the 400's in the stacks?"

WOMAN: "Yes, I found them all right, and I went through most of them, but I couldn't find the language tree in any. I don't suppose there would be any other way of finding it?"

MRS. BERWYN: "No, not that I know of. There are indexes to paintings in books and that sort of thing, but not to a drawing of the kind you're looking for. You know, I'm sure that I've seen that drawing. While you were gone I was trying to think of where, but I just draw a blank. But, if you've tried the language books, then I'd say we just don't have it."

WOMAN: "Well, it wasn't terribly important. Thank you anyway. Goodbye."

How would you comment on the manner in which the reference inquiry described in this case study was dealt with by Mrs. Berwyn? Given the specific circumstances of the case, do you feel that her response was adequate? Had you been in her place, would you have handled the interview differently, suggested other kinds of sources, or carried the search further in some way? Working within the context of the reference sources known to be available at the Lanett Memorial Free Public Library, or which might reasonably be expected to be available there, can you locate a drawing of a language tree such as the one sought by the library patron in this case?

27 A Letter
from an Alumna

Among the mail delivered to the desk of Mary Galena, reference librarian at D_____ College, one morning, was the following letter addressed to the director of the library, Miss Milton:

Dear Sarah,

I am sure you will not recognize my name, but if you will think back to your own undergraduate days at D_____ you may recall Cynthia Casey who lived for two years just a few doors from you in Lewis Hall. I was in the Class of 1927, a year behind you.

Last Spring when I came back to the campus for our reunion, I was thrilled to see the beautiful new library for the first time. How exciting for you! Especially after so many years of having to work in that depressing old Administration Building. As an alumna of D_____, I am proud to have had a part in making it possible.

I was certainly disappointed when I stopped by your office last Spring to learn that you were out of town at a library meeting. We are so far away from the campus it will probably be years before I can convince my husband to make the trip east again. So, I am writing you in the hope that you might be able to shed some light on a little family mystery that has aroused our curiosity.

Two years ago, my husband was clearing out some old family things that had been stored in the trunk for years when we came across a book called, "Aleck, the Last of the Mutineers; or the History of Pitcairn's Island." As you might imagine, I was fascinated to read it, especially with all the current interest in the "Bounty story."

It was published by E. C. Biddle in Philadelphia in 1845.

It does not say who wrote it, but it is entered according to the Act of Congress in 1844 by J. S. and C. Adams. (It is a second edition, so I suppose of no value.)

155

The family interest in it is that it was given to my husband's aunt when she was a little girl as a school prize for perfect attendance. It is signed by a man, probably the school principal.

It seems a curious book to give a little girl, don't you think? Not at all like "I Will Be a Lady" and lives of famous Americans that were the usual gift books. We would love to know its story, who the author was, and something about his life. We have been wondering, ever since we found the book, if it is authentic, or just a made up story. When I was at D——— for the reunion, I saw your wonderful "Reference Room" where the girls study, and I thought that somewhere, in one of those reference books, there might be a clue to his identity.

Fred and I would be so appreciative of any information that you or any-one else at the College could send us. I had thought of writing to one of the Professors, but the faculty seems to have changed so much that I doubt there is one of them who would remember me. Do you remember how frightened we all used to be of them, especially Professor Chester? He was the one with the huge black beard. I suppose he is dead now, he must have been in his sixties when we were at D———.

If you should ever be travelling out St. Louis way, please do look us up. Fred has retired now, and loves to show off his garden.

> Sincerely yours,
> Cynthia C. Eldon
> (Mrs. Frederick G.)
> Class of '27

Attached to Mrs. Eldon's letter was a note from Miss Milton to Miss Galena:

"Mary—I know how busy you are, but could you let me have a few facts about this book and its author? No hurry about it. I will need to have the letter back too, so that I can reply. For the life of me, I haven't the vaguest notion of who Mrs. Eldon is. She must have a better memory than I.— S. V. M."

D——— College is one of the oldest and finest liberal arts colleges for women in the East. Its library contains more than a quarter of a million volumes, and is especially rich in 18th and 19th Century English and continental literature. It has substantial holdings of serials, and in general is quite adequate to support scholarly research in most areas of the humanities and the social sciences. There is an excellent reference collection, including most of the titles one would expect to find in a well-supported university library. The strength of the library is due to the fact that it is well financed by the College, which has a long tradition of scholarship and faculty research. Because D——— is located a considerable distance from any large city, the library has, of necessity, had to develop its collections in sufficient depth to meet the needs of students and faculty for research materials.

The solution of this case consists in the preparation of an adequate statement of biographical information about the author of *Aleck, the Last of the Mutineers* in response to the questions raised in Mrs. Eldon's letter to Miss Milton. Assuming that Miss Galena is a reasonably busy person, it will be important to prepare your analysis with due consideration for the amount of time that can properly be devoted to this particular problem.

28 Contract
Reference Service

The Y_____ Public Library is located in a small city with a population of approximately 30,000 on the eastern seaboard. Y_____ is one of a dozen suburban communities that ring K_____, a city of nearly half a million. Y_____ is a city in transition. A decade ago, it was a minor center for the manufacture of textiles, at that time the chief industry of the region, as well as a residential community for large numbers of unskilled and semi-skilled workers, many of them foreign-born.

About 12 years ago, Y_____ began to change dramatically as the textile plants, under the pressure of foreign competition, were forced to re-locate in another part of the country, because of high labor costs in the northeast. After a severe economic crisis, occasioned by the loss of the city's four largest employers, a citizen's group banded together to lure new industry to the region. Now, Y_____ is again a prosperous, growing community, for textiles have been replaced by new industries, chiefly electronics and plastics. These, in turn, have brought hundreds of highly skilled workers and professional people to the area, many of whom have settled in Y_____. Large portions of the city have changed overnight from farmland to booming settlements of new homes, mainly in the medium and upper-priced brackets.

These changes in the economy and social structure of the community have, in part, occasioned substantial changes in the operation of the Y_____ Public Library. For years, the library had languished under the inept administration of an elderly man, who held his post as a kind of political sinecure under the eyes of a disinterested board of trustees. While the book collection was reasonably adequate in size, it was notably lacking in quality. Little had been added to it in a quarter century except multiple copies of current best sellers, mysteries,

158

westerns and other ephemeral reading. The library building was an unattractive, gloomy example of the worst of late 19th Century neo-classical architecture. In sum, it was a moribund institution, ignored by a majority of adult residents of the community.

Two years ago, the former librarian retired. His successor was Robert Hardwick, a young man who had been born and brought up in a nearby community. After graduation from college, Mr. Hardwick had served briefly in the armed forces, and had then begun a career as a high school history teacher in a rural community several hundred miles from Y_____. After two years, he became interested in the library profession, and decided to change the direction of his career. Since he was unmarried at the time, he was in a position to finance a year of full-time study at a library school to obtain professional training. After a period as an assistant in a large public library in the middle west, he returned to Y_____ to direct the library there. Because his family still lived in the area, and because, for personal reasons, it was desirable for him to be close to them, he was attracted to the position, in spite of the fact that the salary was somewhat less than he might have obtained elsewhere.

In the two years that he has been director of the Y_____ Public Library, Mr. Hardwick has done much to modernize the operation and to improve the quality of service. The budget has been increased to nearly $65,000, which, while still below the level of adequate support, is almost double the amount that was available during the last year of the tenure of his predecessor. Mr. Hardwick has managed to attract a qualified library school graduate to the staff as childrens librarian, although the remainder of the staff is without formal training. Some progress has also been made in convincing trustees and city officials that the existing library building is inadequate, and there has been tentative discussion of an addition, although it is clear that this is still several years away.

Perhaps the outstanding contribution that Mr. Hardwick has made to the library is in the area of public relations. He has set out, almost single handed, to make the city of Y_____ aware of its public library and of the contributions it can make to individual and community life. He has organized a friends of the library group. He has made himself available as a speaker for community organizations, and provided these groups with meeting and exhibit space in the library. He has made extensive use of the local newspaper, both through regular press releases about library activities and through a weekly book review column. One of the banks has cooperated in the publication of a series of attractive, annotated booklists, distributed monthly, describing new additions to the library's collections. All in all, Mr. Hardwick has done an excellent job in terms of beginning to get the Y_____ Public Library back on its feet again, after many years of neglect and lack of support. He is generally well liked by people in the community and by his staff. Although the trustees have been somewhat less than enthusiastic about certain of his programs, they have been reasonably pleased with the results, the most impressive of which has been a substantial increase in the circulation of books.

One evening, as Mr. Hardwick was enjoying a social gathering at the home of the woman who was chairman of his friends of the library group, he fell into conversation with Claude Fenton. Fenton was a man in his middle fifties, who had recently retired as vice president of one of the largest plastics manufacturers in the country for reasons of health. He was generally considered one of the leading citizens of Y_____, a man of substantial resources and social position in the community. Hardwick had been introduced to Fenton once previously at a meeting of a civic group, and he was pleasantly surprised to find, as their conversation developed, that the older man not only remembered him, but seemed to know a good deal about the things he had been doing at the library. Fenton made several complimentary remarks about his work there and indicated that he hoped to have an opportunity to talk with Mr. Hardwick one day soon about an idea he had for further library improvements. Hardwick said he would be delighted to see Mr. Fenton at any time, and invited him to drop in at the library at his convenience.

A few weeks later, Mr. Hardwick received a telephone call from Mr. Fenton, who asked if he would join him for luncheon that day at a downtown restaurant. Mr. Fenton said he had a matter of business concerning the library that he would like to discuss. Mr. Hardwick agreed to meet him, and at the appointed hour found himself seated across the luncheon table from Mr. Fenton. They exchanged casual conversation for a few moments, and then Mr. Fenton began to draw the younger man out on the subject of the Y_____ Public Library. Before long, Hardwick had sketched out, in some detail and with a good deal of enthusiasm, his plans for future library development, and his hopes for either a new building or a substantial addition to the existing one. Mr. Fenton listened with apparent interest, nodding approvingly from time to time, and then said:

"Mr. Hardwick, all of this sounds very exciting indeed, and as I listen to you, I am more and more convinced that the city of Y_____ is very lucky to have a young man of your ability in charge of its library. I think you are going to have that new building of yours one of these days, and this city is going to have a library it can be proud of."

MR. HARDWICK: "That's very kind of you, Mr. Fenton. Of course, I'm sure it is years away, and I can tell you that sometimes I'm afraid a lot of it is just wishful thinking on my part."

MR. FENTON: "Not at all. You can be quite proud of the work you've done here so far, and I'm not the only person in town who thinks so, not by a long shot. Now, if you'll allow me to, let me get down to business with you. I asked you to have lunch with me today because I've been very impressed with the kind of job you've been doing. While you've done many fine things in the time you've been in Y_____, the thing that has impressed me most in my visits to the library is the reference room. Why, the last time I was down there, I noticed that you've even added one of the investment services. I know how expensive those things are, and I'm amazed you could do it with the money you have available."

MR. HARDWICK: "Well, I *have* put a good deal of money into the reference collection, almost $2,000 in the two and a half years I've been here. Of course, we had practically *nothing* in that collection, and most of the money had to go for basic things like encyclopedias, an up-to-date atlas, and periodical indexes. You'd be amazed at how much of our budget was eaten up by about a dozen titles of that kind. Frankly, the investment service, which we just started last month, was a bit of a gamble on my part. It costs over $200 a year, which is a big chunk of my book budget. I put it in because I want very much to promote adult use of the reference collection, and because I'm especially anxious to be able to give some sort of reference service to local businessmen. Part of the reason for this is public relations. I'm sure that you know our local political situation well enough to realize that most of our city officials—our mayor, our city councilmen—are local businessmen. Now, these people are not intellectuals, they're not readers, most of them haven't been inside the library in years. I think it's important that I convince them the library has something to offer them —that it's not just a place for their wives and children to go, but a place where they can get information of the kind every businessman needs from time to time to run his business effectively. I hope to continue every year to add some government documents, directories, and one or two business magazines to the collection, so that some day I'll be in a position to really promote this kind of reference service energetically. I believe that if you want a community to support a public library, then you've got to convince each and every person in the community that the library has *something* to offer him."

MR. FENTON: "I quite agree with you, although I suspect the problem is that you have to invest a good deal in reference books before you're in a position to offer very much service."

MR. HARDWICK: "Yes, that's true. Take the investment service you mentioned a few minutes ago. I'd hate like the devil to have to justify that purchase right now, in terms of its use. I doubt that, at the moment, it's used twice a week. The difficulty is that people in this city just aren't accustomed to thinking of the public library as a resource to turn to when they need facts or information. And, I'm afraid it will take years before they do begin to think of the library in that way. But, of course, the important thing is, when someone *does* come in with a reference question, to have the resources so you can give good service. I think in the long run that's the only way we can attract more customers."

MR. FENTON: "In many respects, it's rather like a man who starts a new business, and is forced to tie up all of his capital in inventory so he can supply whatever his customers happen to ask for. It's a good thing you're not in business. I'm afraid you'd be bankrupt before you had a chance to get started."

MR. HARDWICK (laughing): "Yes, I suppose you're probably right."

MR. FENTON: "Seriously, though, I do see the problem you're up against, and I admire what you're trying to do. I think it's just possible that I may be in a position to be of some help to you. This is what I wanted to talk about with you today. I don't know how much you know about me, but let me explain that up until a year ago, I was in the plastics business. Then, I had myself a spot of coronary difficulty, and I got frightened and decided to retire. I enjoyed my job, and I had a nice income, but these things were not enough to make me want to give up my life for them. Fortunately, I was in a financial position to retire without jeopardizing my family. I'm not a wealthy man, but I could live comfortably without ever working another day, if I didn't want to. I tell you this because I don't want you to misunderstand my motives for having gone back into business again. I've gone back to work, in a very modest way, primarily because I got bored sitting around doing nothing. So, I've gone into the consulting business, under the name of Claude Fenton and Associates."

MR. HARDWICK: "I see. I wasn't aware you'd done that."

MR. FENTON: "Not very many people are, and for the moment I'd prefer, for various reasons, to keep it that way. Our firm has rented an office here in town. Basically, it consists of myself, when I choose to be in the office, and a secretary. I have every intention of keeping this business small, and of treating it rather as a hobby. When a project comes along that interests me, I'll work on it. I may work one day a week, even two days. The rest of the time, I plan to play golf, putter around the garden, or just sleep, if I have a mind to. And some weeks

I don't intend to work at all. The way it operates is this. We have a lot of industry in this immediate area. Every industry, every business has special problems from time to time. I have many friends, and I've discreetly let it be known that I'm available, on a consultant basis, to help solve an occasional problem, if it interests me. Primarily, my own interests and talents are in administrative organization and sales, although I do have a good deal of engineering background as well. And, if I need help on something, I have friends and former associates that I can call on to team up with me."

MR. HARDWICK: "That's where the 'Associates' comes in, I gather."

MR. FENTON: "That's right. Now, to get to where the Y_____ Public Library might come in. From time to time, in the course of this business of mine, I have need of information, or I need to have research done on something. Given the circumstances of my own health and my business, it would be extremely convenient for me to be able to get the information I need, when I need it, from my local public library. I don't think this is too different from the kind of thing you were talking about a few minutes ago, a reference service for the local businessmen."

MR. HARDWICK: "No, it isn't. The only problem is that, at the moment, our resources are pretty limited."

MR. FENTON: "Yes, I know. But, let me give you a few examples of the kind of help I'll be needing. Many times, it will be merely a matter of locating a single fact that I'll have to have in a hurry, like the trade name of a product or the name and address of an officer of some firm. Sometimes it's statistical information I require. Right now, for example, I'm involved with a study of the influence of Japanese-made parts on the radio industry. I'd like very much to have a brief analysis, with some statistics, of the impact in recent years of Japanese tubes on the American market. Let me give you another illustration. Several weeks ago, I was asked by one of the major firms in this area to evaluate several proposals that had been submitted to them by various people to set up a training program for executives using an advanced computer system. You may be familiar with this kind of training program, it's called 'business gaming.' Frankly, this was something quite new to me, and I knew practically nothing about it. A week or so after I finished the job, I happened, just by chance, to be browsing through some old issues of *Fortune* at home, and I came across a perfectly splendid article explaining the whole thing. If I'd had this at hand when I was doing the job, I would have felt a good deal more secure in dealing with the computer boys, I can tell you. Does this give you some idea of the kinds of information that I need?"

MR. HARDWICK: "Yes, sir, it does."

MR. FENTON: "Then let me ask you this. If you had the proper resources, would you know how to find this information?"

MR. HARDWICK: "Yes, I'm fairly familiar with this kind of reference work. I had three years' experience in the business reference department of one of the best public libraries in the country before I came here. It would be largely a matter of having the proper source materials."

MR. FENTON: "Which, of course, is exactly what the Y_____ Public Library doesn't have at the moment, am I right?"

MR. HARDWICK: "That's right."

MR. FENTON: "Now, if you were in my situation, and were going to have regular informational needs of this kind in the future, what would you do?"

MR. HARDWICK: "Well, the answer is, I would set up a library and hire a librarian. But, of course, I realize that wouldn't be practical for you."

MR. FENTON: "Hardly. In the first place, my needs for information will be spasmodic and irregular. Sometimes I'll need to have someone devote as much as a week of solid work to a problem. At other times, I may not need anything at all for several months. So, I've come up with a scheme that I'd like to try out on you for size, a way in which I could make a contribution to the library, while at the same time helping to develop a resource for my own needs. What I should like to propose is that you agree to have the library provide information service for me, when and if I need it. In return, I would be prepared to do two things. First, to make an immediate gift of a sum of money to you for the purchase of library reference books in the fields of business and technology. I would be prepared to make an initial gift of, let us say, $200 for this purpose, and to give at least a like amount every year in the future. This money would be used to purchase books and magazine subscriptions, the titles to be selected by you, to be the permanent property of the library, and, of course, to be available for use by the general public. Secondly, I would be prepared to pay, on a cost-per-hour basis, for such reference service as I would need throughout the year. How does this strike you?"

MR. HARDWICK: "Well, I hardly know what to say. Except that, of course, we would never expect you to make any kind of payment for reference service. As a taxpayer, you're already entitled to that."

MR. FENTON: "Yes, I would agree with you, except that some of my requests for service will involve, I would suspect, a considerable amount of staff time. You can see that, I'm sure, from some of the examples I've given you. I've worked with industrial libraries for years, and I know, for example, that to make a literature search or whatever it is called, on a subject like 'business gaming,' and come up with a list of books and articles, can mean two or three days' work for someone. Now, I just don't see how your library, or any public library, could possibly provide that kind of service to an individual, unless that individual were prepared to pay for it. Secondly, when I do have a need for information, I need it fast, and the one condition of all of this would have to be that you arrange to give a priority to any request I might make."

MR. HARDWICK: "Yes, that would be only fair if you were paying for the service."

MR. FENTON: "Let me just try this out on you for size. A $200 annual gift for the purchase of reference books. For any literature search or other reference job that requires more than 30 minutes of your time or the time of your staff, the library bills me at a rate of, let's say, five dollars an hour. Plus, of course, any expenses you might incur. I would suppose that, at least at the beginning, you might have to telephone other libraries, or even go to them to find material in reference books that you don't have."

MR. HARDWICK: "Frankly, Mr. Fenton, I'm a bit overwhelmed. I've never even heard of a public library doing reference work on this basis, so I wouldn't have the faintest notion of what a fair fee might be. What you've suggested sounds very generous. And, of course, I do see your point about the time that your work would demand. At the M_____ Public Library, where I worked in business reference before I came here, we weren't allowed to take on literature searches or things of that magnitude. The person needing that kind of service simply had to do the searching himself. At Y_____, of course, we just don't have enough reference work of that kind to make it necessary to have such a rule. But, I can see where, if we were to do a substantial amount of reference work for your firm, the problem might arise."

MR. FENTON: "Well, I just wouldn't feel I could ask the library to do this on anything but a paid basis. And, to be quite frank with you, I have neither the time, nor the interest, nor the ability to do it for myself. I wouldn't have the vaguest idea of how to go about it, and at my age, I hardly think it would make sense for me to try to learn, even if I wanted to. If I'm going to work, I'm going to work at something that I know how to do, and leave the library work to professionals like you."

MR. HARDWICK: "Yes, I see your point. Now, if I may, let me try to react to your proposal. First of all, the sums of money you've mentioned seem more than fair, although, of course, I have very little basis on which to judge this."

MR. FENTON: "I know that, and if we were to make this arrangement, I would want it to be subject to review at the end of one year, so as to be sure that the library was being treated fairly. And, frankly, I wouldn't want to be committed to anything for more than a year at a time, because I have no idea at all how long I will want to continue in business."

MR. HARDWICK: "That certainly seems reasonable. Do you have any idea at all of how often you would be calling on the library for reference help?"

MR. FENTON: "As I said, it might be five times in one week, and then not again for three months. That's about all I can tell you. That's why I would want to make our arrangements on a cost-per-hour basis, so that I could feel free to call upon the library as many times as I might need to."

MR. HARDWICK: "I see. I think that I have your proposal, if I can call it that, fairly clearly in mind now. I must confess it does leave me a bit stunned, and I'm just not sure that a library our size could handle it. My first question would be to ask you if it wouldn't be better, from your point of view, to try to work out something like this with the K____ Public Library? The city is only 20 minutes drive from here, and there you have a library that has some trained professional staff, a fair reference collection, and much more in the way of resources than we have."

MR. FENTON: "There are two reasons why I wouldn't want to do that. First, Y____ is my home, and I have a good deal of feeling for and interest in this city. I'd like to make a contribution to it, and this is one way of doing that. I don't have that kind of feeling about the city of K____ or its public library. Secondly, I'm familiar with the K____ Public Library, and I don't think the people over there would understand what I'm talking about. That library is still operating in the 19th century as far as I can see. To my way of thinking, this kind of arrangement depends largely on the individuals involved. I'll be candid with you. I've come to like you, and to admire you as I've had an opportunity to see the kind of work you're capable of. Now, I don't mean for a moment to suggest that you would have to handle this work for me personally, but I would hope you would exercise general supervision over it, and be responsible for it. I'd like to keep this arrangement, insofar as is possible, on a personal basis."

MR. HARDWICK: "Well, to be perfectly honest with you, if we were to take this on, I'm sure that I would have to do most of it myself. One of these days, I'd like to add a trained reference librarian to my staff, but at the moment there isn't much prospect of that. On the other hand, one of the reasons I chose to work in a smaller library is because I like to do a variety of things. I've done this kind of reference work in the past, and I find it quite interesting. I think that when you are interested in something, you can always find the time to do it. I do see some practical problems in your proposal, however, and I suppose I ought to mention them now. Of course, I would have to take this up with the trustees, because I don't have the authority to enter into any arrangement of this kind without their approval. I just don't know how the board would feel about it. I don't know if it's even legal for a free public library to charge a fee for reference service. I'd have to investigate that. The other thing that bothers me is that, under our municipal accounting procedure, any income the library receives has to be turned over to the city treasury, and the library gets no benefit from it."

MR. FENTON: "What about gifts of money? Can't you keep those?"

MR. HARDWICK: "Oh, yes. There would be no problem about the two hundred dollar gift. We could keep that, and spend it for any purpose earmarked by the donor. But, what I was thinking of is the fee for reference service. To my way of thinking, there just wouldn't be any point in our doing this, unless the money were to accrue to the library. The other question I suspect my trustees will ask is whether or not we are prepared to offer this service to other firms in the city. Would you have any objection to that?"

MR. FENTON: "None at all. But, do you think anyone else would want it?"

MR. HARDWICK: "Well, you never know. I doubt it, especially since there seems to be practically no interest among local firms in using our reference service when it's free."

MR. FENTON: "To be quite honest with you, I hadn't really given much thought to your trustees. I had rather hoped this might be something we could work out between us. I must say, I don't particularly relish having my business discussed at a public meeting of the library board. I'll tell you what. Suppose I make my $200 gift for the purchase of reference books to your board, and just leave it at that. Then, suppose we handle the reference work on a personal basis. You bill me, not on behalf of the library, but on your own behalf for any work that you do. I'll make my payments directly to you, and then you do whatever you want with the money. Make a gift of it to the library yourself, or just quietly go out and buy some books for the library with it. In that way, you would avoid all these problems with municipal accounting and with your trustees. My only contact with your board would be as a donor to the library in terms of an annual gift for reference books."

MR. HARDWICK: "Well, I do think it would be more businesslike to do this on a formal, contractual basis, through the board of trustees.

But, what you're proposing might be a better alternative, in view of the mechanical problems involved. I'll tell you what. I'd like to give some thought to this whole matter, not just the mechanics of how it might be done, but the fundamental concept of our providing this kind of service for you. I'm terribly interested in the idea, and I do think it might be very desirable for the library. On the other hand, it *is* brand new to me, and it might lead to complications that I haven't thought of today. I have a trustees' meeting coming up in two weeks or so. May I think this over for a few days, and then talk with you about it again?"

MR. FENTON: "Why, certainly you may."

Assuming that Mr. Fenton is an honest and responsible person, and that he would honor any agreement he might make with Mr. Hardwick or the Y_____ Public Library, how would you evaluate the proposal he has made? What would be the advantages and disadvantages of such a scheme from the point of view of the library? If you were Mr. Hardwick, would you agree to provide reference service to Claude Fenton and Associates on this basis? Must such an agreement be a formal one between Mr. Fenton and the library trustees, or could it be done on a personal basis in accordance with Mr. Fenton's final suggestion?

29 Participation in a Regional Union Catalog

The University of E_____ Library is one of the largest academic libraries in the country, with total book and periodical resources in excess of one million volumes. Located in an urban center, it serves an academic community numbering nearly 15,000 students, faculty, and research workers.

The university is a relative newcomer to the ranks of major American institutions of higher learning, and the library has had to struggle in recent years to keep pace with the rapid growth of its parent institution. The library is housed in an inadequate central building that it has long ago outgrown. The staff is somewhat smaller than it ought to be, and the library administration has been plagued by rapid turnover in personnel at all levels. Merely to acquire, organize, and process the nearly 35,000 items that currently flow into the library each year often seems more than the small staff ought to be expected to cope with. As Dr. Malone, a distinguished medievalist who directs the library, has put it on more than one occasion, "Everything at E_____ is stretched to the bursting point."

The city of Q_____, in which the university is located, is one of the major manufacturing, industrial and business centers of the country. Nearly a million and a half people live or work within its boundaries in a highly diversified industrial and business community. Several large military installations of various kinds are located nearby.

Three weeks ago, Dr. Malone received the following communication written on the letterhead of a local electronics firm's library:

Dear Dr. Malone:

I am writing you on behalf of the Greater Q____ Library Development Committee. On the chance that you may not be familiar with our organization, I should explain that it is an *ad hoc* group of librarians representing 19 public, academic, school and industrial libraries located in or near the city. This group has been meeting together informally for nearly a year in an effort to develop channels of communication between libraries in the region, and improve library services through inter-institutional cooperation. The Committee has now decided to formalize itself, and to sponsor a series of bibliographical projects for the benefit of all members. It has been agreed that our first endeavor along these lines will be to develop a union list of serial publications which, hopefully, will include the journal holdings of all libraries in our region.

I am sure that I do not need to recount to you the benefits of such a union list for all concerned. You, and the members of your staff, have taken a lead, over the years, in stimulating such projects at the national level. Our group feels strongly that the need is just as great locally, especially for some of the newer libraries serving research workers in business and industry. We know the E____ University Library will want to join with us as a co-sponsor of the union list.

This project is, of course, still in the planning stages, and we are hopeful that you, or a representative whom you may designate, will sit in as an *ex officio* member of our executive committee to assist in development of final plans.

The tentative plan calls for publication, in book form, of the complete serial holdings of 41 college and university, public, county, school and special libraries within a 30 mile radius of the city. Each library will be asked to provide, on 3 × 5 slips, a typewritten record of its serial holdings, each title being listed on a separate slip in accordance with a style-sheet now being developed by our committee. Libraries will also be asked to provide cross reference cards for variant titles and corporate authors where appropriate. A committee of volunteers has been formed to take responsibility for editing the slips from reporting libraries, and combining them into a manuscript, which will then be reproduced, according to present plan by photo-offset. We have estimated costs quite carefully, and we are confident that 100 copies of the finished list can be produced for less than $50 per copy. It has further been agreed that participating libraries will be asked to report additions and changes in serial holdings to the committee on a regular basis in the future so that the list can be kept up to date, and regular supplements issued.

This, in brief, is our plan. We are depending on the cooperation and support of every library in our area. Our next meeting is on Tuesday, March 12 at 2 p.m. at the Q____ City College Library. I do hope you can be with us at that time, and that the University of E——— Library will do its part to make our dream of a regional union list a reality.

Sincerely yours,
Evelyn A. Tracy, Librarian
L——— Corporation,
for the Committee

Ten days later, Miss Tracy received the following reply to her letter from John Hopkins, Associate Director for Public Services of the University of E——— Library.

Dear Miss Tracy:

Dr. Malone has asked me to respond, on behalf of the University of E——— Library, to your recent letter to him concerning the proposal of the Greater Q——— Library Development Committee for a regional list of serial publications. Your letter was discussed at length at last Friday's meeting of the library's Administrative Council, which is made up of senior officers and department heads of the university library. It was also considered at a meeting of our faculty advisory committee on the library this morning.

May I begin by saying that we wish you and your committee every success in this undertaking. As you were kind enough to point out in your letter, our library has long recognized the need for inter-library cooperation at all levels, and we have tried to do all in our power to make this a reality. I think the kind of union list you are planning would have real value in improving library services to all. As I am sure you are aware, we are one of the few libraries in this part of the country to report serial holdings regularly to *New Serial Titles,* and we are the only library in the city that participates in the national *Union List of Serials.*

Our participation in these two national projects has resulted in our being deluged with interlibrary loan requests for serials from libraries all over the country. We have been particularly hard hit, in recent years, by interlibrary loan requests of local origin. Insofar as a regional union list of serials might relieve us of part of this burden, we are gratified at the prospect that such a list may come into being.

Regrettably, it does not appear possible for the University of E——— Library to participate in this local project. We estimate that this library currently receives nearly 12,000 items of a serial nature, and that our holdings include many times that number of bound and microfilmed volumes of older serials. To report these holdings, in the form suggested in your letter, or, indeed, in any form, would require an enormous investment of staff time which is far beyond our budgetary capacity in the foreseeable future. Moreover, since our holdings are already recorded in the national union lists, and thus readily accessible for interlibrary loan purposes, it seems to us that to reproduce them locally would represent an unwarranted duplication of effort.

Again, may I wish you every success in this venture which, I know, will greatly strengthen reference and interlibrary loan services in our region.

Sincerely yours,
John Hopkins
Associate Director for Public
Services

Several days later, Mr. Hopkins received the following reply:

Dear Mr. Hopkins:

I cannot tell you how disappointed I and the Committee were to learn from your recent letter that the University of E_____ Library is not willing to participate in the proposed union list of serial publications held by the libraries of Greater Q_____. I am writing you again, at the request of the Steering Committee for the union list, in the hope that you and Dr. Malone will reconsider your decision, for without your participation we feel the project will surely fail.

I do not need to remind you that the University of E_____ Library is the largest in our region, with by far the strongest collections and resources. Indeed, your serial holdings are several times larger than the estimated holdings of all the other participating libraries combined. The libraries in this area need direct and immediate access to these holdings if we are to meet the growing demand of students and research workers for journals.

You speak in your letter of the two national union lists. May I point out that these are so costly as to be beyond the means of many of our local libraries. Moreover, as I am sure you are aware, these lists have serious limitations for interlibrary loan purposes. Certain large categories of serial publications, which we plan to include in our list, are omitted from them. The national lists do not always show the holdings of individual libraries in sufficient detail. Finally, since these lists severely limit the number of locations shown for any given part of the country, they do not show *all* of the holdings of your library. This is exactly why we need the local union list, to supplement the national lists and make up for these deficiencies.

Finally, may I add that of the 41 libraries in our area that were invited to participate in this project, 39 have already agreed to do so. These libraries too face heavy demands on staff time, and yet they are willing to make this sacrifice for the benefit of all. May we hope that the University of E_____ will do the same?

Sincerely yours
Evelyn A. Tracy
for the Committee

Mr. Hopkins' reply to Miss Tracy's second letter is reproduced below:

Dear Miss Tracy:

I have again discussed your letter regarding the proposed union list of serials with Dr. Malone, and I am sorry to report that our original decision against participation in the project must stand. We appreciate the problems you raise with respect to the national union lists and their limitations, but we simply cannot ignore our first obligation, which is to the students and faculty associated with this institution. Since the University of E——— is wholly supported from private, rather than public funds, we cannot allow library services to those outside the university community to impinge on the quality of service to those within it.

Cooperation, Miss Tracy, implies a two-way process. True interlibrary cooperation is not a "one-way street." Yet, when we examine the facts of our own situation, we cannot help but feel that our contribution to the local library community is far in excess of the benefits we receive. To illustrate my point, last year we borrowed about 4,000 items on interlibrary loan, chiefly journals in micro-print and photocopy form. Nearly 90 per cent of these were obtained from other large academic libraries or from the Library of Congress. Only about ten per cent came from libraries in our immediate area. On the other hand, we loaned last year almost 7,000 items to other libraries, and more than half of these were sent to libraries within a 30-mile radius of this city. I am sure you will agree that we have made a substantial contribution locally.

From these statistics alone, you can see that, for us, interlibrary loan tends to be a losing proposition, since we lend far more than we borrow. I know you are also aware of the fact that the lending of books in this way is expensive, since it involves staff time in verifying bibliographical data, locating the item, preparing it for shipment and the like. Fortunately for us, most of the requests that have come to us in the past from public and school libraries in the area have been for monographs, which we lend in their original state. Periodicals, however, are another matter. Here, we cannot lend originals, and since many of the local libraries do not have the equipment to handle microfilm, we must prepare photocopies. If these libraries should begin to ask us for journals in greater numbers, as they surely would if our holdings appeared in a local union list, our costs would rise to the point where they could only be termed prohibitive, and we might well be forced to curtail these services drastically.

We can avoid this only if other, smaller libraries in the area are willing to share the burden of interlibrary loans. To the extent that your proposed union list will help make this possible, we are strongly in favor of it and hope that it will materialize in due course. I know that you and the members of your committee will appreciate our situation and will understand why we cannot take part in the project.

Sincerely yours,
John Hopkins

Assuming that the content of these letters is an accurate reflection of the local situation with respect to interlibrary loans, how do you evaluate the positions of Mr. Hopkins and the University of E____ Library on the one hand, and Miss Tracy and her committee on the other? Do you feel that the University of E____ Library is obligated to participate in the local union list of serials? What further arguments might be advanced in favor of each side in this controversy?

What general problems of interlibrary cooperation are reflected in this case study? What steps has the library profession taken to alleviate these problems?

30 An Unknown
Sourcebook

Joan Preble, young adults librarian at the R_____ Public Library, was surprised to find Louise Cromwell standing in the reference room at 3:30 in the afternoon. Miss Cromwell is children's librarian at R_____, and it is indeed unusual to find her anywhere but in the children's room at that time of day. As Miss Preble joined her, Miss Cromwell began their conversation in the following manner:

MISS CROMWELL: "Joan, are you the person on duty in the reference room this afternoon?"

MISS PREBLE: "Yes, today's my day at the desk. But, how is it that you're able to be up here? Have the children gone on strike or something?"

MISS CROMWELL: "Oh, no. We have the usual afternoon crowd downstairs. I just came up for a minute, on the run, to find out if I might be able to get some help from someone here. I've got a very strange reference problem down there that I don't have any notion of how to handle. But, you look so busy that I hate to bother you."

MISS PREBLE: "Well, it's been a little hectic for the last half hour or so, but things seem reasonably calm at the moment. Is there some way I can help you?"

MISS CROMWELL: "I hope so. I have three youngsters down at my desk, fifth graders from the A_____ School. They've been given a homework assignment for tomorrow by their teacher, a Miss Ely. I'm sure I don't know who Miss Ely is, but I gather she's a new teacher who doesn't live here in R_____. I tried to telephone her at the school, but apparently everyone there has gone home for the afternoon. You see, these three children have just come in, and each of them has been given a different name. Each child is supposed to find out a few facts about the name he's been given."

MISS PREBLE: "It sounds reasonable enough so far."

MISS CROMWELL: "Oh, yes, but wait until you hear the names —Martha Dandridge, Arnold Cream, Frances Gumm—have you ever heard of any of those people?"

MISS PREBLE: "No, I don't think so. Who are they?"

MISS CROMWELL: "Well, I know who one of them is. It was just a good guess on my part, but I thought I recognized the name 'Martha Dandridge.' 'Martha Dandridge' was Martha Washington's maiden name. But, I don't have the vaguest idea of how you would find that out, or where you would go to look it up, if you didn't happen to know it, do you?"

MISS PREBLE: "No, I don't. Do you think 'Frances Gumm' is someone's maiden name too?"

MISS CROMWELL: "Not that I know of. And 'Arnold Cream' certainly isn't. Now these children tell me their teacher told them there's a book in the library that has all of these people in it. I've looked through the card catalog under 'names,' and I can't find a thing. Do you know if we have any reference book that might have that kind of information?"

MISS PREBLE: "Not offhand. I can't think of anything like that. Certainly not in the young adults' collection. Could it by any chance be in the children's room?"

MISS CROMWELL: "I know every book in the children's collection, and I'm sure it isn't. What's bothering me, beyond the immediate problem of these three children, though, is the fact that apparently we'll have 25 or 30 others with the same kind of problem before the afternoon is over. I just don't know how to handle it."

MISS PREBLE: "The same problem, but with different names, I suppose."

MISS CROMWELL: "Yes. Each child has been given a different name to look up, as I understand it. Joan, I know Mrs. Ludlow doesn't like to have small children upstairs in the reference room, and I see that the room is pretty full right now. What would you suggest I do? I don't know how to help these children. Shall I just turn them away? Do you think you could help them, if I sent them upstairs to you?"

The R_____ Public Library is a small one, serving a suburban, residential community of about 20,000. The book collection numbers approximately 40,000 volumes, of which almost half are juveniles and books for young people. The reference collection consists of about 300 volumes and includes the *Reader's Guide to Periodical Literature*, the

Cumulative Book Index, the *Dictionary of American Biography, Current Biography,* the *National Cyclopedia of American Biography* (permanent volumes only), *Who's Who in America,* recent printings of the *World Book, Encyclopaedia Britannica, Encyclopedia Americana, Collier's Encyclopedia,* the *Dictionary of American History,* all the volumes in the "Famous First Facts" series, and the usual assortment of atlases, statistical annuals, almanacs and special biographical dictionaries that one would expect to find in a small public library. The professional staff includes Mrs. Ludlow, the director of the library, Miss Preble, Miss Cromwell, and an adult services librarian who happens to be off-duty at the present time. The reference room serves both high school students and adults, and on a reasonably busy afternoon, such as the present one, it is not unusual for the person on duty to handle 100 or more inquiries of various kinds during a three-hour period.

If you were Miss Preble, what advice would you give Miss Cromwell with respect to handling the problem described in the case study? How would one go about identifying Arnold Cream, Frances Gumm, and similar names, bearing in mind that this must be done within the framework of resources that are either known to be available, or might reasonably be expected to be available in the R_____ Public Library?